How to Help your Child
at Primary School

If your child is at Primary School (or starting soon), you'll probably have noticed a few changes to school life since you were a bright-eyed young learner.

Not to worry — this CGP book is packed with advice to help you parent your way through Primary like a pro. We've covered the social and practical sides of school, from settling in at the start to coping with assessments in Year 6.

There's also plenty of in-depth info about all the subjects your child will be studying, so you can help with those tricky homework questions without missing a beat!

How to access your free Online Edition

Contents

Choosing a Primary School

Preparing your Child for School

Health & Wellbeing

What Will My Child Learn at School?

Testing & Assessment

Preparing for Secondary School

Published by CGP

Editors: Sharon Keeley-Holden, Christopher Lindle,
    Sam Norman, Megan Pollard

Contributors: Amanda MacNaughton, John Svatins

With thanks to Katie Fernandez for the proofreading.
With thanks to Jan Greenway for the copyright research.

ISBN: 978 1 78908 838 0
Printed by Elanders Ltd, Newcastle upon Tyne.

Based on the classic CGP style created by Richard Parsons.

Primary School — an overview

So, you and your child have survived the world of Nursery and now it's time to take the big leap into primary school. Here's a brief run-through of what's in store...

Primary school in England

Things are _different_ outside of England:

- In _Wales_ they have the same structure but _don't have SATs_.
- In _Northern Ireland_, the key stages are _structured slightly differently_ and they also _don't have SATs_.
- _Scotland_ has a _different system_ altogether.

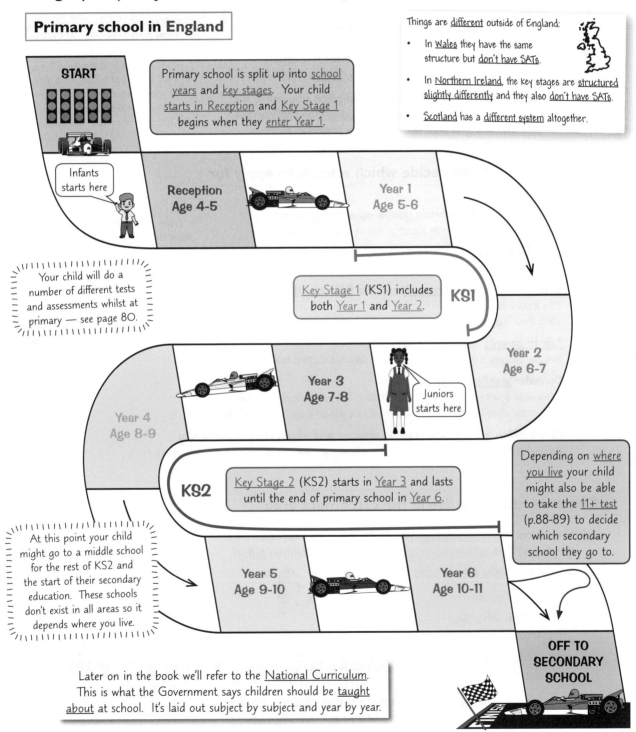

START

Infants starts here

Primary school is split up into _school years_ and _key stages_. Your child _starts in Reception_ and _Key Stage 1_ begins when they _enter Year 1_.

Reception Age 4-5

Year 1 Age 5-6

Your child will do a number of different tests and assessments whilst at primary — see page 80.

Key Stage 1 (KS1) includes both _Year 1_ and _Year 2_.

KS1

Year 2 Age 6-7

Year 3 Age 7-8

Juniors starts here

Year 4 Age 8-9

KS2

Key Stage 2 (KS2) starts in _Year 3_ and lasts until the end of primary school in _Year 6_.

Depending on _where you live_ your child might also be able to take the _11+ test_ (p.88-89) to decide which secondary school they go to.

At this point your child might go to a middle school for the rest of KS2 and the start of their secondary education. These schools don't exist in all areas so it depends where you live.

Year 5 Age 9-10

Year 6 Age 10-11

OFF TO SECONDARY SCHOOL

Later on in the book we'll refer to the _National Curriculum_. This is what the Government says children should be _taught about_ at school. It's laid out subject by subject and year by year.

Getting your Child into School

Almost a full year before your child starts Reception you need to choose and apply for a school place. This process can sometimes be stressful, which is why we've gathered plenty of useful information for you.

The application deadline is 15th January

1) In England and Wales, children normally start Reception in the <u>September following their fourth birthday</u>.

> If you don't think your child will be ready to start school by then, you must still apply at the usual time, but can request a later start date. However, your child must be in full-time education at the beginning of the term after their fifth birthday.

2) For the best chance of getting the school place you want, it's vital you don't miss the <u>15th January deadline</u> for applications, so start considering school options in the previous autumn.

Do your research to decide which schools to apply for

- **Read up about the schools you're considering <u>online</u>**
  This'll give an idea of what's on offer, e.g. special clubs and sports teams.

- **<u>Visit</u> the school (e.g. on open days)**
  This can give you an idea of whether it'll suit your child.

- **Check out the <u>Ofsted reports</u> and the <u>SATs results</u>**
  Take these with a pinch of salt though — a change in staff, for example, can affect these 'snapshots' greatly. You can find these on the gov.uk website.

- **<u>Talk to parents</u> of current pupils**
  This can give you a feel for what the school is like, but it's best to seek several views.

- **Consider <u>practical stuff</u>**
  Think about how easy it'll be to get your child to and from school every day, and also whether the school's before and after-school care will work with your schedule.

- **Check which schools are <u>realistic choices</u> and which are pie in the sky**
  Each school's admissions criteria (see below) will help you see how likely you are to get a place there.

> In Wales and Northern Ireland you have the added consideration of whether you want a Welsh/Irish or English speaking school for your child.

"Stop moaning Jack. The SATs results at this school are excellent."

Check whether you live in the catchment area

1) If a school is <u>oversubscribed</u> (there are too many applicants for its places) then <u>admission criteria</u> decide which children get in.

2) Schools typically give <u>priority</u> to:

- Children in <u>care</u>.
- Children with <u>siblings</u> already at the school.
- Children who live <u>closest</u> to the school.

> A school's <u>catchment area</u> varies each year. You can often get information about the previous year's catchment area from the local authority website.

> It might be tempting to use a friend or relative's address for the school application, but <u>don't do it</u>. It can result in your child <u>losing their place</u> at a later date — and with an oversubscribed school there will be plenty of people keen to <u>blow the whistle</u>.

3) Many people assume that attending the <u>school nursery</u> will help their child get a place in Reception, however, it usually <u>doesn't</u>.

Getting your Child into School

Faith schools often have extra requirements

<u>Priority</u> for faith school places is usually given to children whose parents are members of a particular religion. You usually have to 'prove' this somehow, e.g. by having a vicar confirm you've been attending church regularly. So, if you're taking up a religion just to get a school place then it may take considerable advance planning and commitment...

Stay awake Beth, or we won't get into St Cuthbert's.

> Some parents want their child to go to a faith school because the teaching will match their <u>religious beliefs</u>. However, faith schools often <u>perform better</u> than non-faith schools, so many non-religious parents are also keen for their child to get into one.

Fill in the application form with your preferences

You can usually apply <u>online</u> on your local authority's website. You'll be asked to list <u>between three and six choices</u> (depending on your area) in <u>order of preference</u>.

- <u>Don't</u> put just one school down.
  It doesn't mean you'll definitely get in, and you may end up being offered a place at the least popular school in the area.
- **Make sure that one of your choices is a school that you'll** <u>almost certainly</u> **get a place at.**
  This protects you from being offered a place at an under-subscribed school that you really don't want.
- **Schools** <u>don't find out</u> **where you put them in your order of preference.**
  You'll be offered a place at your highest preference school that you're ranked highly enough for, depending on the admissions criteria. So if you don't make the cut for your first choice, you might be offered your second choice over someone who put that school as their first choice.

I promise I'll run loads of bake sales.

16th April — primary school offer day

You'll most likely <u>receive an email</u> telling you which school you're being offered a place at. If it's your first choice school, great, but if it's <u>not a school you wanted</u>:

- <u>Don't reject it</u> — there's a risk that your child will end up with <u>nowhere to go</u>.
- Join the <u>waiting lists</u> for schools that you'd prefer — these lists <u>stay active</u> through the first term, in case any children leave, and you can check your position on a list at any time.
- You can <u>appeal</u> — you should get a letter telling you how. You'll have to show that the admissions criteria were <u>applied incorrectly</u> (e.g. they measured the distance to your house wrongly), or that the school you want would meet your child's needs <u>much better</u> than the one offered (e.g. your child has a documented speech problem and your preferred school has a special speech therapy unit).

It's not all about the SATs results...
A school might get outstanding results by making pupils spend the whole of Year 6 preparing for the tests. It's important to look at the bigger picture, e.g. art, music, outdoor education, as well as values and pastoral care.

Practical Skills

Children can be at very different stages when they start school. Some struggle to do their coat up, while others are busy putting up shelves...

Ideally they'll be able to do some things for themselves...

GO TO THE LOO

We all know this one's a big deal. Your child needs to know how to <u>wipe themselves</u> properly and <u>pull up their underwear</u>. It's important they know to <u>flush the toilet</u> and <u>wash their hands</u> afterwards too.

If your child has accidents from time to time it's a good idea to let their teacher know and pack spare underwear in their school bag.

EAT WITH A KNIFE AND FORK

This is particularly important if your child will be <u>having school lunches</u>. There'll be supervisors on hand to help, but they can't help all the children at once.

Besides, little Edwin/Edwina will feel more confident if they can <u>cut up their own food</u>.

GET DRESSED

If your child can fasten and unfasten buttons, zips and Velcro, they'll be able to <u>go to the toilet without help</u> and <u>change for PE lessons</u>.

EVENING RITUAL

Help your child get into the habit of getting their uniform and school bag ready <u>every evening</u>. It'll help the mornings feel less rushed.

Before their first day at school have a practice run of getting ready. It'll prepare you both for the big day and might even generate some excitement.

Make sure they know how to ask for help

- Children need to know that the adults at school are <u>there to help them</u> when they find something difficult.

- Teaching your child to <u>ask for help</u> when they need it is really important. Teach them that they should <u>put up their hand</u> if they want to get their teacher's attention.

"I learnt the hard way to make sure my son knew to <u>let go</u> of the bread when feeding the ducks. Thankfully, just as the river started to carry him away a helpful stranger retrieved him from the river for me..."

— Dippy

CONFESSION CORNER

What did the plate say to the knife and fork? Lunch is on me...

The most important thing is to try not to worry. Your child may not be able to do all these practical things straight away, but that's completely normal. With help from you they'll become confident in doing them in no time at all.

Social Skills

It's really important for your child to develop good social skills during their school years. Fear not though, here are some things you can do to help your child on their way to becoming a social butterfly.

Having good social skills will help your child settle in more quickly

⭐ ASKING FOR WHAT THEY NEED

Your child needs the confidence to communicate their needs, e.g. to ask if they can go to the toilet or ask another child if they can borrow something. Make sure your child feels comfortable asking for things that they need.

⭐ LEARNING TO SIT STILL

Children will have to sit still and listen at school. They're much more likely to manage this if they have got used to doing it at home first. Getting them to do this whilst you read them a story might be a good way to practise.

⭐ TAKING TURNS AND SHARING

Being able to take turns and share is essential. Help your child to develop these skills by playing games with them that involve taking turns and encouraging your child to share their toys when they have play dates.

⭐ DEALING WITH LOSING

Some children find it hard to lose (some adults too...) so it's helpful if they've had this experience before starting school. Help your child by playing games where they're not always the winner. Even if it's through gritted teeth, encourage your child to congratulate others when they win.

⭐ PLEASE AND THANK YOU

Remind your child to use good manners with their teachers, friends and at home.

If your child struggles with some of these skills, don't worry — it can take time to adjust to school life. If you're really worried, speak to your child's teacher and ask their advice.

Children learn social skills through play

Children will be given lots of opportunities to play when they start school. It really helps if they have ideas for playground games.

Give your child some ideas like make-believe, running races or making up a dance.

Language and Communication

From birth, your child will have used their voice and body language to make sure their needs were met. As they get older, language becomes increasingly useful to them as a way of communicating.

Good communication skills are vital

- They help children form and understand relationships with others.
- They allow children to have their needs met, and let others know how they feel about things.
- They include listening and understanding, which are needed for learning.

You can help your child develop communication skills

Children should hear about 21,000 words every day to develop language skills, so you should talk, talk and talk some more — but do let your child speak too.

Studies have found that the more words young children hear, the better they're likely to do when they start school.

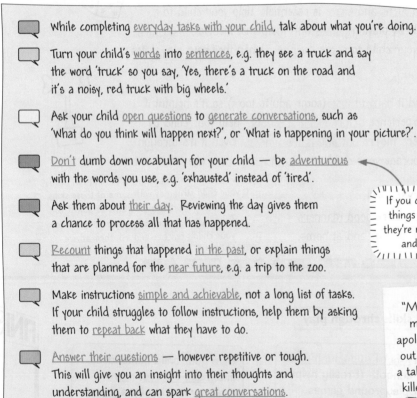

While completing everyday tasks with your child, talk about what you're doing.

Turn your child's words into sentences, e.g. they see a truck and say the word 'truck' so you say, 'Yes, there's a truck on the road and it's a noisy, red truck with big wheels.'

Ask your child open questions to generate conversations, such as 'What do you think will happen next?', or 'What is happening in your picture?'.

Don't dumb down vocabulary for your child — be adventurous with the words you use, e.g. 'exhausted' instead of 'tired'.

Ask them about their day. Reviewing the day gives them a chance to process all that has happened.

Recount things that happened in the past, or explain things that are planned for the near future, e.g. a trip to the zoo.

Make instructions simple and achievable, not a long list of tasks. If your child struggles to follow instructions, help them by asking them to repeat back what they have to do.

Answer their questions — however repetitive or tough. This will give you an insight into their thoughts and understanding, and can spark great conversations.

Caitlin's mum shrieked the open-ended question, 'Why did you do it?'

If you do this when talking about things your child is interested in, they're more likely to pay attention and absorb the new words.

"My child's teacher once met me in the playground and apologised for my loss. It turns out my daughter had invented a tale about her grandma being killed by an alligator whilst on a cruise..."

CONFESSION CORNER

— Ali

Language and Communication

Teach your child emotional intelligence

1) Children who are able to <u>connect with their feelings</u> and <u>express them</u> tend to perform better <u>academically</u>, have better <u>relationships</u> and be able to <u>manage conflict</u>.

2) You can help your child develop their emotional intelligence by:

- Helping them to <u>recognise their feelings</u> by teaching them words such as happy, excited, frustrated, jealous, to <u>label</u> them with.

- Show them <u>empathy</u> by saying things like 'You must have felt frustrated when...', or 'I understand why you are feeling so angry...'.

Lin had really set her heart on a doughnut...

- Demonstrate good ways of <u>expressing your feelings</u> — they're likely to be influenced by the way you do this. For example, say things like 'I'm disappointed because the cafe has sold out of cake' or take deep breaths if you're feeling stressed or angry. Hopefully expressing their feelings will avoid them resorting to a tantrum...

Create opportunities for language and communication

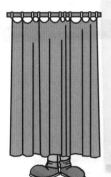

Play <u>games</u>, especially those with <u>simple rules</u>, e.g.

- <u>I Spy</u> using colours or initial sounds.
- <u>Hide and Seek</u> to use language like 'I wonder where they are', 'Are they behind this curtain?', 'I think they might be under the bed.'
- <u>Simple board games</u>, such as snakes and ladders.
- <u>Memory games</u>, e.g. you say 'I went to the shop and bought an apple', then your child follows with 'I went to the shop and bought an apple and a banana'. Repeat in <u>turns</u>, adding on one extra item each time.

Being able to take turns is an important skill to learn. It'll help your child at school, both in the classroom and in the playground.

Go to <u>playgroups</u>.
This allows your child to:

- practise their <u>negotiation skills</u> with other children, e.g. about sharing a toy.
- see you communicating with <u>other adults</u>.
- <u>sing songs and action rhymes</u>, which you can repeat at home.

Get involved when they're playing with <u>Lego</u>® or Play-Doh®. Activities like these will generate <u>conversations</u> about what they are making and how to share things.

Role play with them, e.g.

- Set up a <u>shop</u> with pretend food.
- Have a <u>dolls' tea party</u> or <u>picnic</u>.
- Play <u>pretend nursery</u> with toys.

Mum, why does that lady have a hairy chin?

When your child is at school, they'll spend half their time being told not to talk, and the other half being encouraged to talk. When they're at home, give them lots of chances to talk, and do your best to show interest.

Reading to your Child

It might seem like everything has gone digital, but books still play an important part in school life. As well as giving your child a head start, developing a love of reading can be really enjoyable.

Making books and stories part of everyday life

- Build reading a story into a routine, e.g. a story at bedtime.
- Stick your feet up and let your child see you reading a book.
- Go to the library so your child can choose some books to borrow for free.

- Read in fun places, e.g. a den made from blankets.
- Give books as birthday presents. It shows you value them.
- Keep books in your bag or the car. Read them while waiting for the bus or for the rain to stop.

EMBRACE TECHNOLOGY

- Download some books on a tablet — handy for packing light when going on holiday.
- Look up kids' books on YouTube. There are stacks of them being read aloud. They're free and are perfect for when you're cooking etc.
- Use audiobooks, maybe in the car, at bedtime or when children are playing quietly.

Charity shops are a good source of cheap books (and you don't have to remember to return them).

Listening to audiobooks develops comprehension skills and vocabulary — and it hasn't been found to delay reading development.

TEACH READING SKILLS AT STORY TIME

- Point to the words as you read them. Your child will learn that the blocks of letters relate to words, and that we read from left to right.
- Show them how to choose a book by looking at the covers, or by looking for books by a particular author.

VARY WHAT YOU 'READ'

- Read poetry, comics, magazines and information books — it all counts.
- Try books with no words, e.g. *Tuesday* by David Wiesner. Your child can make up the story to go with the pictures.
- Tell stories about your child, e.g. of the day they were born, or the day they started nursery.
- If you're even vaguely imaginative, make up stories for your child. They may want to get involved with how the story develops.
- Some young children enjoy being read a chapter book over several days — useful if you've also got an older child. Try *Flat Stanley* by Jeff Brown, or *My Naughty Little Sister* by Dorothy Edwards.

The 'You Choose' books by Pippa Goodhart and Nick Sharratt are books of pictures and no words that can prompt discussions.

If only there was some way that Shabnam could keep her daughter entertained when she was using both the phone and the laptop.

Read it again, Daddy (and again and again and again)...

Your child will almost certainly have phases where they insist on the same book being read to them over and over (and they'll definitely notice if you try to sneakily skip a few pages). However, repetition has been shown to be great for building vocabulary. And with any luck, the ritual of reading that book might send them off to sleep.

Helping your Child Learn to Read

You don't need to try to teach your child to read before they start school. However, there are some things you can do at home to prepare your child for learning to read at school.

Build on what they learn at pre-school

Your child's pre-school or nursery will have provided lots of different <u>activities</u> and an <u>environment</u> which has taught your child that <u>words tell them something</u>. Your child will have done things such as:

Painting Corner

- Listened to and discussed <u>stories</u>.
- Participated in <u>rhyming games and chants</u>.
- Identified <u>labels and signs</u> in their environment.
- Learnt some <u>letters</u> of the alphabet, making <u>letter-sound matches</u>.
- Used <u>known letters</u> to try <u>writing</u>.

Things you can do at home

<u>Reading books</u> to your child is the obvious way of helping them get off to a great start, but other things include:

Point out <u>letters</u> and <u>words</u> in the environment, such as <u>signs</u>, <u>shop names</u>, <u>labels</u> on food and packaging, etc., and read them with your child.

Label their toy boxes so they begin to <u>recognise words</u> that relate to what they play with, e.g. puzzles, cars, building blocks, etc.

Claire was going to label the toy boxes, but realised the labels would all need to say 'random tat'.

<u>Label</u> things that <u>belong to them</u>, like their bag and shoes, with their <u>name</u>. This is useful for starting school as it means they can <u>identify their peg</u>, etc.

Sing <u>songs</u> and <u>rhymes</u>. This helps them hear the <u>syllables</u> and <u>sounds</u> words are made from — a vital skill for starting <u>phonics.</u>

Pin up the <u>letters of the alphabet</u> in their bedroom. You can buy a poster or find one online to print off.

Have <u>magnetic letters</u> on the <u>fridge</u> or <u>foam letters</u> in the <u>bath</u> that they can play with.

Let your child watch <u>Alphablocks</u>, a CBeebies programme with fun and friendly <u>letters of the alphabet</u> who work together to make words and tell stories using <u>phonics</u>.

Help them to <u>read the cards</u> they receive on <u>special occasions</u>.

Use different materials like <u>sand</u>, <u>paint</u> and <u>chalk</u> to practise marking out <u>letters of their name</u>.

Helping your Child Learn to Read

Playing with sounds prepares your child for reading

For info about Phonics see pages 31-32.

Helping your child to distinguish the sounds in words will stand them in good stead for learning Phonics.

Challenge your child to think of as many rhyming words as possible for words such as cat, back and sky.

Nonsense words that rhyme are good too — e.g. dat, lat. It's the rhyming pattern that's important.

Make up your own rhymes, e.g. instead of 'Miss Polly had a dolly who was sick, sick, sick...', you could sing 'Mr Bar had a car, that was fast, fast, fast...'.

Read books written in rhyme, and pause before reading the final rhyming word so that your child can predict it.

Make up alliterative phrases (ones in which an initial sound is repeated, e.g. pretty pink pig) to describe things such as toys or food.

Why, thank you!

Encourage your child to make different sounds in front of a mirror, such as 'th' and 't', so they can watch how their mouth and tongue move.

When you're making letter sounds for your child, try and say 'sss' rather than 's-uh', and 'mmm' rather than 'm-uh', etc.

When reading stories, encourage children to join in with repetitive phrases, e.g. 'I'll huff and I'll puff and I'll blow your house down'.

Games are a fun way of helping your child

1) There are lots of games you can buy to help your child recognise letters, words and sounds, e.g. lotto. Alternatively, you can make your own:

Play magnetic fishing with letters or known words written on the fish. If your child can read what's on the fish, they get to keep it.

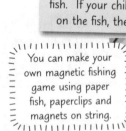

You can make your own magnetic fishing game using paper fish, paperclips and magnets on string.

Play Pairs by writing letters or words on pieces of paper — you need two pieces with each letter or word on. Place the pieces of paper face down, then take it in turns to turn two over, read them and if they match, keep them.

Play I Spy using initial sounds. You can make it easier by placing a selection of objects with different initial sounds on a tray.

2) There are lots of reading apps you can download, e.g. *Teach Your Monster to Read* or *Reading Eggs*. These teach basic reading skills through games — just don't let your child stay on them all day.

Relax and enjoy seeing your child's reading improve...

Children develop at different rates, so don't worry if your child has no interest in letter sounds and just wants to play energetically. Even if your child is capable, don't push too hard, or they may start to dislike learning.

Teaching your Child about Maths

Just by playing with their toys, your child will be exploring maths concepts, such as size and shape. There are some other things you can do to help them prepare for maths at school too.

Five skills that will prepare your child for maths at school

Go on a number hunt around the house, or when out and about. You'll spot numbers everywhere, from wheely bins to the backs of football shirts.

When out shopping, count the number of items you put in the shopping basket or trolley.

Play board games with dice, such as snakes and ladders or ludo.

1. Counting out loud — forwards and backwards.
2. Recognising the digits 0 to 9.
3. Use words to do with size, e.g. small, tall, thick.
4. Recognising simple patterns.
5. Knowing basic shapes such as lines, circles, squares and triangles.

Let your child play with a pegboard so they can explore patterns.

Allow them to watch TV programmes such as *Numberblocks* (on CBeebies) or *Numberjacks* (see YouTube) and talk about what they see.

Talk about the shapes of their toys using language such as round, curved, flat, sides, straight and corners.

Read books that involve counting, e.g. *Counting Creatures* by Julia Donaldson.

Be warned, baking with a child never looks this neat and tidy.

Get your child involved with baking — they can count out cake cases, or cut out biscuits using shaped cutters.

Sing songs that involve counting, such as: '1, 2, 3, 4, 5, Once I caught a fish alive', 'There were ten in the bed', and 'Five little ducks went swimming one day'.

Maths is fun — make that your mantra...

Even if you found maths tough as a child, or just simply hated it, it is really important that you say positive things about maths. Although, with most of these activities your child won't even realise they're doing maths anyway.

Parent Survival Tips #1

You're basically your child's backstage crew, responsible for all the props and costume changes. There's a lot to deal with so the next few pages are about preparing yourself for your child's school days.

Get ready for party invites

1) Starting school brings with it a <u>stream</u> of invites. You'll give up <u>many Saturdays</u> taking your child to their <u>latest social event</u>, e.g. a party in a community centre with a hired princess/superhero.

2) While your child is young, you'll have to <u>stay there</u>, making <u>small talk</u>, until it's time to take your sugar-hyped, over-tired child home again.

3) Try these <u>tips</u> to get through the early years.

> Don't despair. As your child progresses through primary school, the parties become fewer and you can just drop and dash.

PHOTOGRAPH INVITES

Doing this as soon as your child brings them home means you'll have the <u>details</u> should the invite get <u>lost</u>.

HAVE A CARD/GIFT STASH

- Buy a stash of <u>birthday cards</u>, and rolls of <u>gender-neutral gift wrap</u>.
- Put <u>duplicate</u> and <u>unwanted gifts</u> your child receives in a 'present box'. When they're off to a party, just <u>pull one out</u>. (Just don't re-gift it to the person they got it from.)

GO PREPARED

- Take a <u>book</u> to read (or a <u>large newspaper</u> if you really don't want to chat).
- Take <u>spare clothes</u>. Excitement can cause even the most reliable child to have an <u>accident</u>.

DON'T ASSUME SIBLINGS CAN GO

- Chances are there <u>won't be enough</u> food boxes, party bags, craft supplies, or the entertainer might charge <u>per head</u>.
- At a <u>soft play</u>, you might be able to pay for the sibling, but prepare them for not being allowed to dine at the party table.

It's easy to get sucked into <u>competitive party throwing</u>. Don't. Set a budget and <u>stick to it</u> — the kids will have a great time regardless. Just because the last few parties had a bouncy castle, mobile disco, magician and a face painter, doesn't mean yours has to. In fact, a <u>gazebo</u> in the <u>park</u> would make a lovely change.

School uniform tricks

1) Don't put the school T-shirts in the 'T-shirt drawer', and the bottoms in the 'bottoms drawer'. Stick all their uniform <u>together in one place</u> and your child can pull out what they need each morning.

2) Do a '<u>uniform wash</u>' and save having to sort it out. If your child wears <u>coloured shirts</u>, even better — there's no fear of <u>dingy grey whites</u>.

WIN THE ODD SOCK BATTLE

- Buy loads of <u>identical pairs of socks</u>. Grab any two, and you have a pair.
- When you're <u>putting socks away</u>, make a <u>game</u> of it by racing your child to pair up the <u>most socks</u>.

Frozen wedges of lemon and lime are great for gin and tonics...

And if you want to be able to eat those nice chocolates or biscuits yourself, then hide them in an empty coffee tin.

Types of Parent

Your child isn't the only one meeting new people when they start school. Unless they're in breakfast club and after-school club every day, you'll stand around in the playground with a bunch of other parents twice a day.

Spot these parent types

THE COMPETITIVE ONE

This parent is likely to start a conversation with you about <u>reading book levels</u>, because they want to check that their child is on a <u>higher one</u> than yours. No matter what <u>out of school activity</u> you sign your child up for, this parent will be there, because their child does them <u>all</u> — and <u>excels</u> at each of them. They'll definitely try to get you to follow them on <u>social media</u> so you can see their child's <u>latest triumphs</u>.

THE ALWAYS LATE ONE

Can be spotted hurrying towards school at <u>9:02 am</u>. The other parents wonder why they don't just set their alarm <u>10 minutes earlier</u>. Their child is usually sat in the school office at the end of the day <u>waiting to be collected</u>.

THE SPORTY ONE

Always dressed in <u>sports gear</u>. They drop their child off and <u>jog off</u> down the street. <u>Not</u> to be confused with parents that just dress in active wear because it's <u>comfy</u> for <u>watching TV</u> in.

THE PTA ONE

On <u>first-name terms</u> with all the teachers as they've pretty much lived at the school for the last six years due to having several children. They're always sending WhatsApp messages asking for <u>bake sale donations</u>, etc. If their child ever <u>wins</u> anything all the other parents suspect preferential treatment. Teachers are just glad of the <u>free labour</u>.

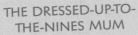

THE TRENDY DAD

He'll be in his <u>tight jeans</u> and shades, convinced that all the mums <u>fancy him</u>. Likely to work 'in media' from home, meaning he can do the school run every day.

THE DRESSED-UP-TO-THE-NINES MUM

It might only be 8:45 am, but this mum is <u>perfectly made up</u> wearing the latest fashions. She'll often be accompanied by a <u>dog</u> of the fashionable breed of the moment.

Other parents — they're just regular people like you...

It's easy to be intimidated by the other parents at pick up. They might all seem to stand around in cliques, making you feel like a reject. Don't take it personally, smile pleasantly and focus on real life away from the school gates.

Parent Survival Tips #2

Primary schools are always throwing fundraisers at you. For example, you may have to send your child with £1 to dress in something spotty (time to scour the racks for something that's spotty enough...).

Cheat at cake making

There'll always be one parent who never fails to make a show-stopping cake for every bake sale. Even if you're the world's worst baker, here are a few ways to produce your own 'home-baked' wonder that every child wants a slice of.

GET FRUITY

For a no-skill bake sale wonder, slather any plain shop-bought cake in whipped cream and strawberries. It'll be delicious and count towards your five-a-day.

GO TALL

This cake will stand head and shoulders above the rest. Buy several plain chocolate cakes and stack them up separated by big splodges of buttercream and maybe chocolate spread or jam too. A chocolate bar cut in half and wedged into some icing on the top completes the look (and you can eat the other half).

Alternatively, you could mix it up a bit and alternate chocolate and vanilla cakes.

BE PREPARED

Keep some plain fairy cakes in the freezer and some tubes of icing in a range of colours in the cupboard. Now you're ready to make cakes to match any theme thrown at you, even if you've totally forgotten until you wake up that morning.

Good old chocolate crispy cakes are a speedy option to make from scratch. Don't limit yourself to the classic cornflakes or rice crispies — it's a fab opportunity to get shut of that cereal that your kids loved last week but now won't touch.

EMBRACE SWEETS AS TOPPINGS

Arranging any sort of sweet treats on a cake makes it look amazing and distracts from dodgy decorating.

You can even make a 'piñata' cake by hollowing out the middle and filling it with sweets before decorating it.

Don't forget the stash of cash either...

You may hardly ever use cash these days, but a cash-free primary school is a rarity. Keep a stash of pound and 50 pence coins to send with your child when needed. Though you might have to keep it well hidden to stop anyone 'borrowing' some for parking. It'll also save you having to send a fiver and hoping in vain for some change.

Sleep and Routine

Like everyone, young children need sleep and it's really important they get it (both for them and for you). Sometimes getting them to sleep is tricky, but a predictable routine can help.

Sleep and a good routine go hand in hand

It's pretty obvious that a child who is getting enough sleep is more likely to be <u>happy</u> and <u>alert</u> than a child who isn't. Getting your child into a good sleep pattern <u>isn't</u> just about avoiding tantrums though, lack of sleep has been linked to future problems, such as <u>anxiety</u>, <u>depression</u>, <u>obesity</u> and <u>high blood pressure</u>.

HELPING THEM SLEEP

- Have a predictable <u>routine</u> to help children <u>relax</u>, e.g. a warm bath, a story, then bed.
- Use <u>blackout blinds</u>, or improvise by sticking heavy paper or tinfoil to the window.
- <u>Turn off screens</u> an hour before bedtime. <u>Audiobooks</u> or good old <u>paper books</u> are good alternatives to eBooks.
- If you've tried everything and your child still has trouble sleeping, then talk to your <u>GP</u> or <u>health visitor</u>.

HOW MUCH SLEEP?

As a rough guide, children need:

1-2 year olds — 11 to 14 hours of sleep
3-5 year olds — 10 to 13 hours of sleep
6-12 year olds — 9 to 12 hours of sleep

Light from screens stops the production of the sleep hormone melatonin, so it can affect natural feelings of sleepiness.

Cho's parents couldn't understand why she was so tired when she got 14 hours sleep a night.

GIVING UP THE DAYTIME NAP

Children generally <u>give up</u> having a nap between the ages of three and five. If your child is about to start school but <u>still</u> has a nap, it can be worrying.

- Try replacing naps with '<u>quiet time</u>', e.g. where they look at books, in the same place each day.
- Talk to your child's <u>teacher</u>. Yours won't be the first child to struggle to get through the day without a nap. Reception classrooms often have a <u>quiet area</u> where children can <u>rest</u>.

Raheem was adamant that quiet time was not required.

GET INTO A GOOD ROUTINE

Children <u>benefit</u> from routines — knowing what's coming next makes them feel <u>secure</u>.

Starting school often means a <u>change in routine</u>, so it's worth thinking about it in advance:

- Get <u>prepared</u> the night before. Your child can help you set out their <u>uniform</u> and pack their <u>bag</u>.
- Set the <u>alarm</u> so you have plenty of time to do everything in the morning, and maybe even a peaceful coffee before your child wakes up.
- Be prepared for <u>tired</u>, <u>hungry</u> children after school — a <u>snack</u> in your pocket may save the day.
- Build in time for <u>reading</u>, <u>stories</u> and <u>conversations</u> about how your child's day went (they may not be receptive to this immediately after school though).

I can only find one shoe — and I have jam in my hair...

You can't plan for every last minute crisis, but building extra time in to the morning routine will help. Make a habit of checking through the messages from school — it's easy to forget that empty yogurt pot they need.

Food and Drink

To get through the long school day, your child is going to need some sustenance. The exact routines and rules vary between schools, but here's some general information to be going on with.

There is such a thing as a free lunch

Under the Government's Universal Free School Meals scheme, Reception, Year 1 and Year 2 children are entitled to a free school lunch.

However, your child may be eligible for Free School Meals (FSM) for all of their time at school depending on your financial circumstances. The school will ask you about this before your child starts school.

The School Fruit and Vegetable Scheme (SFVS) provides a free piece of fruit or vegetable each day for every child in Reception, Year 1 and Year 2.

The school will tell you how to make sure your child gets this.

The Nursery Milk Scheme entitles under fives to a third of a pint of milk each day.

If your child goes to breakfast club, they'll have food such as cereal and toast on offer. Also, after-school clubs will usually offer a snack to keep the children going until they get home.

You can usually choose a school dinner...

I said I wanted a ham sandwich as usual.

1) School lunch menus are usually available online (often through an external provider). You choose what you want your child to be served each day.

2) There's often a hot dinner, a vegetarian alternative, and a sandwich or jacket potato. There are occasionally special theme days too, e.g. Chinese New Year.

3) When your child gets to Year 3, you'll have to pay for the lunch — usually around £2.50 a day (unless you're entitled to Free School Meals).

Encourage your child to try out different foods from the menu.

...or send a packed lunch

Packed lunches are ideal for picky eaters, and can work out cheaper. The only downside is, you have to make them...

- Schools often have rules about packed lunches — sweets are usually banned, and often chocolate and crisps too.
- Some schools are 'nut-free' zones (due to children with allergies). This means you have to be careful to avoid foods containing nuts, such as chocolate and hazelnut spread.

In most primary schools, drinking water throughout the day is now the norm. Your child will probably need a bottle labelled with their name.

School dinners — no longer concrete chips and soggy semolina...

If your child has food allergies, it's worth talking to the school to see if they can provide a safe lunch. You should also warn your child not to share someone else's lunch too.

Bonus Tips — Packed Lunches

If your child takes a packed lunch, the same old sarnies can get a bit boring after a while. Not to mention the tedium of making it every day. Try some of these ideas to brighten up your child's lunchtime.

Get creative

1) Assuming you have plenty of <u>time</u> on your hands, adding <u>faces to food</u> is guaranteed to make your child <u>smile</u>.
   If you don't have enough time, or the inclination to faff about making faces, be thankful you don't live in <u>Japan</u> where your child's packed lunch is expected to be a <u>work of art</u>.

2) You can buy special <u>icing eyes</u>, or improvise with <u>olives</u>, <u>raisins</u>, <u>marshmallows</u>, or a tube of black <u>writing-icing</u>. For <u>glue</u>, try cream cheese or ready-made cake frosting.

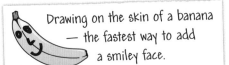

Drawing on the skin of a banana — the fastest way to add a smiley face.

Hopefully your child is open to the resulting interesting flavour combinations.

- A faster way to make a packed lunch more fun is to use <u>cookie cutters</u> to cut sandwiches into <u>shapes</u> such as <u>hearts</u> and <u>stars</u>.
- You can <u>slather the offcuts with jam</u> and have a <u>well-deserved snack</u> (or freeze them for breadcrumbs). Waste not, want not, so they say.

3) If you're feeling really keen you could even add a <u>joke</u> for them to read and tell their friends.

What do you give to a sick lemon?
Lemon aid.

Why don't eggs tell jokes?
They'd crack each other up.

Lots of websites have printable jokes that are specially formatted for a lunch box. (I know, I couldn't believe it either.)

Some bonus practical tips

KEEP IT COOL
<u>Freezing</u> a carton of juice or a pouch of yoghurt will work as an <u>ice pack</u> and keep everything chilled until lunchtime.

COMPARTMENTALISE
You can buy lunch boxes with <u>separate compartments</u> — or you can use silicon or paper <u>cake cases</u> to separate each type of food. As well as making the lunch look more <u>tempting</u>, you use <u>less</u> non-recyclable cling film.

KEEP APPLE SLICES FRESH
Apple slices are often more <u>appetising</u> than a full apple, but go <u>brown</u> if left to their own devices. If you slice the apple then <u>hold the slices together</u> with an <u>elastic band</u>, they'll stay fresh.

Whole apples — they survive 12 trips to school before needing to be replaced...

If your child doesn't actually eat the fruit you put in their lunch box, but you feel the need to include some anyway (just in case the school staff use it to judge your parenting abilities), then this is the fruit of choice.

School Life

School life can be a bit of a whirlwind, even for the parents. There are a lot of things to remember...

Watch out for communications from school

1) With most schools, hunting through your child's bag for a letter about an event is a thing of the past. Schools typically use a <u>communication app</u>, such as ClassDojo.

2) These are great for:

- <u>Informing parents</u> about everything from special events to parking rules.
- Sending a message to you about <u>your child</u>, e.g. about a minor injury.
- <u>Showing</u> parents what their child has been up to through <u>photos</u> and <u>videos</u>.
- Allowing <u>you</u> to send <u>messages</u> to teachers about your child.

Mrs Little

It's National Fruit Day tomorrow, so please send your child in an appropriate costume. A donation of £1.50 is expected. Sorry for the short notice.

Don't expect an instant reply to your message, particularly if out of school hours — some teachers have lives.

3) Parents will often set up an <u>unofficial social media group</u> for a particular class or year group. This is really handy for <u>queries</u> that you don't want to bother the teacher with. However, if you have a <u>complaint</u>, always take it directly to the school — posting negative things on social media can land you in <u>hot water</u>.

It's not all about the lessons

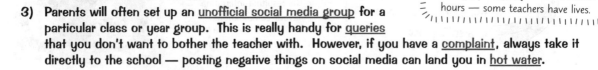

SPECIAL DAYS

- Some of these happen every year, e.g. <u>World Book Day</u>. Others might be a one-off related to a topic, e.g. World War 2 day.
- Irritatingly for parents, they'll generally involve a <u>costume</u>. <u>Advance planning</u> is key here if you want to avoid staying up all night crafting, or paying a fortune for next-day delivery (see p.20)
- Search the internet, especially parenting forums, for <u>easy, cheap ideas</u>.

I really want to be an astronaut, but my mum forgot so I have to pretend that I want to be a teacher.

SHOWS AND CONCERTS

- Primary school productions range from the standard <u>nativity</u> to <u>Shakespeare plays</u>.
- They'll often be organised so that each child has at least <u>a line or two</u>.
- You might be asked to produce a <u>costume</u> for your child to wear in the show.

EXTRA-CURRICULAR ACTIVITIES

- These can give your child the opportunity to learn something a bit <u>different</u>, from chess to street dance.
- They're <u>not</u> free childcare though. Usually a particular teacher has volunteered to run one, and so they may be <u>cancelled</u> with short notice. Also, forcing your energetic child to do meditation classes for your convenience won't end well for anyone.

School Life

SCHOOL TRIPS

- These vary from a simple walk to the post office for Reception, to a trip abroad for Year 6.
- Whatever the trip, make sure you return the signed permission form promptly.
- Read what they need to take carefully and don't be tempted to break the rules, by letting them take a secret phone or extra spending money.
- If your child gets travel sick, give them medicine when you drop them off, and warn the teacher.

There should be a dedicated member of staff who's responsible for medication — they'll collect in and hand out any that children might need during a trip.

Trips are usually beneficial and enjoyable for children, but they can sometimes be expensive.

- If the trip takes place within school hours, you may be asked for a 'voluntary contribution', but your child can't be left behind if you don't pay. However, if not enough parents pay, the trip may be cancelled.
- Other trips can be charged for. If you're struggling to pay for a trip that your child wants to go on, then it's worth asking the school for help at an early stage.

If your child receives Free School Meals then they'll also get 'pupil premium'. This is extra funding that the school can use to pay part of the cost of school trips as well as other extra-curricular activities.

I am so going to win again this year.

DROP OFF AND PICK UP

- Don't try to drop your child off too early — for older children in particular, it may result in an unsupervised stand in the rain.
- Teachers will usually sign young children out at the end of the day, noting who collects them. If they're going home with someone who isn't a parent or guardian, make sure the school knows about it otherwise they won't let your child leave.
- You might want your older child to gain some independence and start walking home without you. Make sure you inform the school that you give permission for this to happen.
- Some families might be entitled to free transport if it is too far to walk or unsafe to walk to school. Your local council website will have more information.

Hey, weren't you meant to be going to after school club today?

SPECIAL PROJECTS

- Your child is likely to have to do some special projects during their primary school years. Perhaps one of the classics like making a fruit solar system, a Tudor mansion, or the Easter favourite, a scene featuring decorated eggs.
- Whether you delight in such tasks or not, you're likely to have to find appropriate materials, e.g. loo rolls, yoghurt pots and egg boxes.
- Try not to do the task for your child. The teacher won't be fooled — they know that even the brightest 7-year-old can't make a working volcano with lights and sound effects.

You miss the memo and send your child in school uniform on Pirate Day...

It's a parent's nightmare. There are a lot of plates to keep spinning, especially if you've got more than one child. A calendar may help you keep track — or a checklist stuck to the front door of what they need each day.

Bonus Tips — Fancy Dress

World Book Day is the big dress up day at primary — although some schools do reduce the stress by decreeing that all children should just come in pyjamas that day (if so, check they put underwear on...).

You could just nip to the supermarket...

1) However, your child will most likely be one of twenty kids wearing the <u>same costume</u>.

2) Also, if there's a <u>prize</u> up for grabs, a shop-bought costume will <u>never</u> win.

3) It's also <u>not a green choice</u> as these costumes are usually <u>destined for landfill</u> after one wear — most charity shops won't take them because they're often <u>super-flammable</u>.

4) So, if you want your child to <u>stand out</u>, and <u>save the planet</u> in the process, you basically have <u>two options</u>...

1 Spend hours crafting and sewing a thrifty and sustainable costume

1) Imagine — an eco-friendly *enormous* caterpillar costume from <u>recycled cardboard boxes</u>, painted in shades of green.

2) It's definitely a <u>potential winner</u> that will make your child stand out from the crowd. However, it might prove such a pain to make that you end up <u>dashing to the supermarket</u> anyway.

3) If you do manage to cobble something together, <u>congratulations</u>, but be prepared for <u>moans</u> as your child wiggles their way across the playground with bits of cardboard <u>poking them</u>.

2 Work with what you've got in the house*

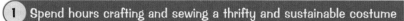

Find a book to match the costume

- If you've got a <u>witch costume</u> lying around — then how about Meg from *Meg and Mog*? A <u>skeleton costume</u>? It's got to be *Funnybones* by Janet and Allan Ahlberg.

- With a <u>pirate outfit</u> you could go classical with *Treasure Island* — or add <u>underpants</u> for *Pirates Love Underpants*.

Accessorise, accessorise
Normal clothes with...

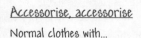

- ...a <u>bucket</u> and <u>toy dinosaurs</u> = *Harry and the Bucketful of Dinosaurs*

- ...a cardboard <u>golden ticket</u> = *Charlie and the Chocolate Factory*

- ...a <u>saucepan</u> and a <u>wooden spoon</u> = *George's Marvellous Medicine*

Make colour work for you

- Green clothes + red hat = *The Very Hungry Caterpillar*
- Blue clothes + white bandages = *Mr Bump*
- Blue dress + white tights = *Matilda*
- White clothes + black spots drawn on = *101 Dalmatians*
- Black shorts + red top with black = *Dennis the Menace* duct tape stripes

Go with questionable literature
You may feel that <u>superheroes</u> and <u>Disney Princesses</u> aren't characters in 'real books', but there are books featuring them, so go with it.

* These things <u>only work</u> if your child <u>doesn't</u> have their heart set on being a <u>particular character</u>. It might be a good time to teach them the <u>art of compromise</u> if they do...

Homework

The dreaded H-word. Schools vary in how much they set, but your child will almost certainly get some.

Make homework part of your routine

1) Some children <u>love</u> homework, whereas others will come up with <u>any excuse</u> not to do it, and before you know it, it's bedtime.

2) If there's a routine children follow each day after school, they'll know what's <u>expected</u> of them, and the homework is more likely to get done. Consider <u>writing</u> it out and sticking it to the fridge.

Fronted adverbials? They're worse than long division. Is 4:30 too early for wine?

SET UP A HOMEWORK AREA

- Find a <u>quiet</u>, <u>distraction-free</u> place where your child can do their homework each time.
- <u>Switch off</u> the TV and check there's <u>enough light</u>.
- Make sure <u>everything needed is at hand</u>, so no time is wasted hunting for a pencil sharpener.

Reading, spelling, times tables — the bread and butter of primary homework

READING

- <u>Little and often</u> is best — e.g. 10 minutes a night for young children.
- <u>Talk</u> to children about what they've read, and how they felt about it.
- <u>Don't</u> cover the pictures, even if your child relies on them heavily.
- If your child <u>misreads</u> a word, let them read on — they may <u>self-correct</u>.
- Don't <u>pressure</u> your child to progress through the reading scheme. Build up their <u>confidence</u> on easier books.

SPELLING

Get your child to practise their spellings <u>every night</u> so they have time to sink in. Try these <u>strategies</u> to help your child learn tricky words:

- Highlight the tricky bit for your child to focus on, e.g. fri<u>e</u>nd.
- Look for words within words, e.g. there's a rat in sep<u>a</u>rate.
- Say it how it is <u>spelled</u>, e.g. Wed-nes-day.
- Make up a <u>mnemonic</u>, e.g. to spell rhythm remember <u>R</u>hythm <u>H</u>elps <u>Y</u>our <u>T</u>wo <u>H</u>ips <u>M</u>ove.

TIMES TABLES

<u>Quick recall</u> of times tables helps with lots of maths topics. Here are some ways to help your child get them learned:

- <u>Fill time</u> with times tables, e.g. when waiting for a bus.
- Find a <u>fun video</u> on YouTube for the table being learned.
- Focus on just <u>three</u> tricky facts for a few days, e.g. 6×7, 7×7 and 8×7.
- Practise using an <u>app</u>, or a game on the <u>internet</u>.
- Teach your child some <u>tricks</u>. E.g. for the 4 times table you can use 'double then double again'. So, to work out 3×4, double it (6), then double it again (<u>**12**</u>) — $3 \times 4 = 12$.

Don't do their homework for them...

But do help them — it sends the message that their learning is important. In Maths particularly, try to help children use the methods they're asked to use, even if they'd get the answer faster using a different method.

Friendships

We all remember what it was like — 'BFF's one minute, sworn enemies the next. Fortunately there are some things you can do to help your child make friends, and keep them...

Ways to help your child form friendships

 Help them develop friendship skills

- Practise taking turns, e.g. when playing a game at home.
- Praise them when they do something caring or considerate. This will be more successful than pointing out when they get things wrong.
- Role play situations, e.g. breaking the ice with a potential new friend.
- Be a role model for what makes a good friend, e.g. you could involve your child when you do something kind to help out a friend.

Ah, that's OK. But touch my pencil again and you're dead.

Provide opportunities to form friendships

- A play date at their home should help a shy child feel more confident. Suggest ways they can be a good host, e.g. by offering their friend a drink, and help them choose some games in advance.
- Groups, such as Beavers, also give children chance to make friends in a structured environment.

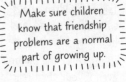

Having a craft or baking activity prepared can give the play date structure and reduce the pressure on your child.

If your child says they have no friends

- Acknowledge their feelings. Saying "I see you're feeling lonely", rather than, "Of course you have friends", helps them feel more understood.
- Don't overreact. There's a good chance that everything will be fine the next day.
- Talk to their teacher — they may be able to pinpoint a problem that you can work on with your child, or they may have an idea how to smooth the path for them.
- Make suggestions (or even better, encourage your child to come up with ways to solve the problem). For example, perhaps your child is pursuing a friendship with someone who isn't interested, but there are other children who would be.

Make sure children know that friendship problems are a normal part of growing up.

Remember, fallings out are usually temporary...

Children usually patch things up quite quickly, so be wary of wading in and complaining to another parent. There's a real danger that you'll turn a small disagreement into something larger.

Bullying

Sadly, bullying is something that exists in all walks of life. School should always be somewhere where a child feels <u>safe</u> — if you suspect bullying is a problem this page will provide some information about what to do.

What is bullying?

1) Bullying is <u>repeated</u> behaviour that aims to hurt someone. It can take different forms, from name calling to hitting. Bullies exploit an '<u>imbalance of power</u>' like <u>strength</u> or <u>popularity</u> to hurt someone.

2) Children who experience bullying may be reluctant to speak and may express their worries through <u>uncharacteristic behaviour</u>. Be alert to your child being 'a bit off' and give them time to share their feelings. Take care to avoid asking <u>leading questions</u>.

> Leading questions encourage a particular answer. For example, asking 'Is Ruby is always nasty to you?'.

Listen carefully to your child

1) Once they feel comfortable enough to speak freely, give them time to explain what is happening. The most important thing is that they <u>feel listened to</u> and that they understand that they <u>deserve to be treated well</u>.

> Keep a <u>record</u> of what your child tells you — this may be important if you need to talk to the school.
> Log all <u>future incidents</u>, and take <u>photos</u> of any damage to property, etc.

2) It might be hard not to feel angry about the situation, but children often feel very <u>anxious</u> about talking and they need you to <u>be calm</u>. Don't be tempted to confront the bully or their parents — it can make matters worse.

Other things you can do to help

Talking with your child about how they might <u>respond differently</u> to bullying could help them. Being <u>assertive</u> without being <u>aggressive</u> is a good life skill and may mean they are seen as less of a '<u>soft touch</u>' by future bullies.

If <u>nasty messages</u> are being sent by social media or text, teach your child how to take a <u>screenshot</u>. Cyberbullying is <u>increasingly common</u> for primary age pupils and a screenshot can be <u>important evidence</u>. Also, show your child how to <u>block</u> the bully from sending messages.

> To use social media apps you must be at least 13 years old, but it's not unheard of for younger children to have accounts. For more, see page 25.

Work with the school to make things better

1) The first step is to approach the class teacher in a <u>non-confrontational</u> way. In the large majority of cases, bullying can be fixed <u>quickly</u>, such as by talking to the bully, or by changing groupings.

2) Every school has a <u>behaviour policy</u> that includes measures to prevent bullying. This means that the school should already have strategies in place to help.

3) If the bullying <u>continues</u> and you aren't happy with how it is being handled, the next step is to write to the headteacher. Hopefully this will resolve things, but if not, there are ways of taking it <u>further</u>. These steps can be found on the websites of organisations such as BullyingUK.

4) Some parents feel that <u>moving schools</u> is the only solution. However, it should be a last resort as settling into a class where everyone knows each other comes with its own difficulties.

Screen Time

Screens are a huge part of life these days. Children are surrounded by people constantly checking their phones, and with streaming services and watch on demand, there's always something fun to watch on TV.

Not all screen time is bad

SCREEN USE CAN BE BAD...

- An obvious one, but using a screen a lot means you're <u>less physically active</u> which can lead to <u>obesity</u> and other <u>health problems</u>.
- Family members spend <u>less time interacting</u> with each other.
- It can <u>affect your sleep</u> as light from screens can stop you feeling sleepy (see p.15).
- High screen use has been linked to <u>behaviour and attention problems</u>.

Screen use can lead to increased snacking.

...BUT SOME SCREEN USE CAN BE GOOD

Some studies have found that up to <u>two hours</u> a day of screen time (TV or devices) can actually be <u>beneficial</u> for children, especially if it's for <u>certain activities</u>, e.g.

- Watching well-designed <u>educational</u> programmes.
- Playing computer games which involve <u>interacting</u> with friends (either in the same room or online).
- <u>Video calls</u> with family and friends, or being read a story remotely.

Get your child into healthy digital habits

Be a good role model
Make time for screen-free activities and let your child see you doing them.

Set time limits for screen use
For example, 30 minutes in the morning and an hour after school.

For example, Google's Family Link™ parental control app and Apple's Screen Time app.

Use device settings to limit screen time
Devices offer loads of parental controls. E.g. make it so that you have to 'approve' new app installations, and that inappropriate content is filtered out. Some apps can be set as 'always allowed', while others can be disabled at certain times. On a phone, they won't affect your child's ability to contact you though.

Sam thought that getting a pet would reduce screen time. He was right.

Make some family rules
E.g. no screens at the dinner table, in bedrooms (particularly overnight), or too close to bedtime.

There's more about apps on the next page.

I don't want a pony — I want a new phone...

Many children get their own phone in the later years of primary school. You might want your child to have one when they start walking to school alone, or meeting friends in the park, or because you don't want them to be left out socially. Whatever the reason, stay one step ahead of them and stick to any ground rules you set.

Staying Safe when using Apps

These days it's inevitable that children will have access to various apps, perhaps even those for social media sites. After reading this page you should be clued up and prepared to help your child to use them safely.

There are loads of different apps out there

It can be <u>hard to keep up</u> with all the apps that are available out there, so here's a quick guide to some different types.

1 **Messaging apps, e.g. WhatsApp**

These are popular as messages can be sent for <u>free</u> when on WiFi. However, there's a risk of <u>inappropriate content</u> and <u>cyberbullying</u>.

2 **Self-destructing message apps, e.g. Snapchat**

These can be <u>dangerous</u> as they can encourage children to send things they wouldn't want <u>hanging around online</u>, such as embarrassing photos and nasty messages. However, <u>screenshots</u> can be taken.

3 **Photo and video sharing apps, e.g. Instagram and TikTok**

Children may view <u>inappropriate content</u>. Also, studies have found that children link their <u>self-worth</u> to their number of '<u>likes</u>' and '<u>followers</u>'.

4 **Chat apps used when online gaming, e.g. Discord and console-specific chat platforms**

Children are likely to chat to people they <u>don't know</u>, exposing them to anything from <u>swearing</u> to <u>inappropriate conversations</u>.

> Some game apps have built-in chat features.

Some of the most popular apps are for <u>social media sites</u>. Although primary school children are <u>too young</u> to have their own social media accounts, many do and parents are often under pressure to let their children 'join in' so they aren't left out.

13+ **16+** Social media apps have <u>minimum age limits</u>, although they're often not hard for tech-savvy children to get around. Ignoring them means your child is likely to see content <u>inappropriate</u> for their age.

Help them to use apps safely

1) Different apps pose <u>different potential dangers</u> to a child. E.g. gaming apps for young children should only contain appropriate content and are unlikely to allow messages to be sent between users. However, it's a good idea to <u>check this out</u>.

2) Here are three steps to help <u>keep your child safe</u>:

> Make sure your child knows they can talk to you or another trusted adult if they see something online that worries or upsets them.

1. <u>Talk</u> to your child about what they're doing online and <u>explore</u> the apps <u>together</u>.

2. <u>Agree</u> some <u>rules</u>, e.g. they'll <u>ask</u> before downloading a new app, and that they'll let you <u>check their device</u> when you ask.

3. Use <u>settings</u> to help keep your child safe.

BE ALERT TO ONLINE DANGERS

- Make sure your child knows that they should <u>never share</u> information such as their <u>name and address</u> online.

- Show your child how to <u>block</u> anyone who posts things that upset them, or strangers that try to make contact.

- Get the lowdown on the latest apps from the <u>NSPCC Net Aware website</u>. For each app, it tells you how to use the <u>settings</u> to protect your child, and also things to talk to your child about so they are alert to <u>dangers</u> related to the app.

Diversity in School

(Spoiler alert) Not all the pupils are going to look and sound like your child at school.
(Another spoiler alert) At school your child should treat others with respect and expect the same back.
(Yet another spoiler alert) There are no more spoiler alerts on this page.

Schools have a diverse mix of children

In your child's school there are likely to be children who are
different from your child. For example, they might:

- be from a different ethnic background.

- follow a different religion.

- have a physical or learning disability.

- speak a different language and
be learning English (see below).

- be transgender.

Of course, your child might fit with one or more of the above.

Cheese...

Children are taught about diversity and respect

A classroom environment should make every pupil feel comfortable to
help build their self-confidence. Your child's school will probably:

- have clear ground rules about respectful speech.

- give assemblies on themes such as friendship, diversity, equality and racism.

- use books and display posters around the school that show diversity.

- raise awareness of diversity at certain times of the year,
such as Black History Month, Diwali and Chinese New Year.

- cover some of these topics, such as friendships, in PSHE (see page 79).

> Your child's school
> will probably have
> an Equality Policy
> to read on their
> website if you want
> to find out more.

Children with EAL* get extra support

It's important to let your child's school know if they speak another language
at home — even if your child is fluent in English. The school can help by:

- teaching them lots of vocabulary in preparation for what they'll learn
in different subjects, e.g. providing them with vocabulary mats.

- adjusting activities so the language is more accessible.

- arranging English language teaching time — this might
take place with a Teaching Assistant in small groups.

> Being able to speak another
> language is an amazing
> skill and the teacher will
> probably want to celebrate it
> with the class. For example,
> they may ask children to
> respond to the register in
> their own language — e.g.
> 'Bom Dia senhora'** instead
> of 'Good morning, Miss'.

If you're concerned, speak to the school...

Well... perhaps not the school itself — but the teachers that work in it. Whatever the issue, they'll probably have
come across something similar before and have sensible ideas to deal with it to be able to put your mind at rest.

*English as an Additional Language
**This is Portuguese, I'm reliably informed.

Relationships and Sex Education

In primary school it's compulsory for children to be taught relationships education but not sex education. However, many schools choose to teach some aspects of sex education to their pupils.

Relationships Education

1) The purpose of relationships education is to teach children about various aspects of positive relationships. These include their relationships with friends, family members and other adults and children.

2) Much of relationships education can be taught as part of PSHE (page 79) and other subjects but some schools will teach it separately. Either way, here are some examples of things that your child will learn.

Being Safe

- About boundaries in different friendships.
- The importance of privacy but also to not keep secrets if they relate to someone's safety.
- What is and isn't appropriate contact with another person and how to react to and report inappropriate behaviour.
- Asking for advice or help if they feel unsafe and to keep trying until they receive it.
- Where to get advice from.

Online Relationships

- How to keep safe online — this includes how to spot harmful content or communications and how to report them.
- That the same rules they use in-person also apply online, such as manners and respect.
- How to critically consider what they see online and their online friendships — not everything they see will be true and people may not be who they say they are.
- How people's data and information is used and shared online.

Families

- That not all families look the same — parents could be the same sex, families may have a single parent, grandparents may be filling the 'parent role', foster parents and carers could be involved, etc.
- That a stable family usually has strong and caring relationships at its core and that this is important for supporting a child as they grow up.
- How love, security and stability are important to a family. Through this, your child will learn to recognise a family relationship which has none of these and how to ask for help or advice if they need to.

Caring Friendships

- How to make and choose friends.
- That a friendship should make them feel happy and secure.
- The characteristics of a healthy friendship.
- That lots of friendships will have ups and downs but often the downs can be worked out rather than letting them ruin a good friendship.
- Working out who to trust and not trust and that friends should not make you feel uncomfortable.

Respectful Relationships

- They should respect other people and expect the same in return.
- Being polite and courteous to other people.
- About bullying (see pages 23 and 25).
- What a stereotype is and how these can be a negative thing.
- That they need to seek and give permission in all relationships.

Jonah had to explain to his mum that LOL didn't mean Lots Of Love....

Relationships and Sex Education

Sex Education

1) At primary school all children are taught about topics relating to sex education as part of Science and PSHE. This includes how the human body changes during puberty, the emotional changes that take place during puberty and how some plants and animals reproduce.

2) As it's not compulsory, there's not a set list of things for schools to cover — it's up to the school to decide. Below are some of the sorts of things your child may learn about.

The school should contact you with the details of what they intend to cover on sex education before teaching begins. You have the right to withdraw your child from any sex education that isn't on the National Curriculum for Science.

Puberty

Greater detail about aspects of puberty, such as:

• hair growth in new places.

• how boys' voices change.

• growing pains and how certain areas might become sensitive, such as the chest area.

• teaching them about good personal hygiene habits.

• periods and how to cope with them using pads and tampons.

Usually girls are given a talk about periods by a female teacher or the school nurse. There might be a chance for girls to submit questions anonymously to be answered in this talk. Boys are also taught about periods, usually separately from the girls.

Reproduction

More about reproduction than the coverage of the basics in Science. For example:

• the different ways you can have children, such as traditional pregnancy, IVF, adoption or surrogacy.

• the emotional impact of pregnancy and the decisions needed to become parents (by any means).

• the different body parts that play a role in reproduction.

Children can start puberty when they are at primary school

Primary schools tend to teach some sex education because some children will start puberty in Juniors. Making sure they're prepared is important, especially for girls, who can begin their periods during primary. Here are a few things to bear in mind:

1) You might notice that your beloved child's mood or attitude starts to change when they get to Juniors — a cause could be the start of puberty.

2) Hormones begin to fly around your child's body and can cause these changes before any physical manifestations occur.

3) It can be quite a scary time for children as their bodies and moods change. Growth spurts, acne, periods, wet dreams and extra hair growth can be a lot for them to deal with.

4) So it can be helpful to make sure your child knows they are able to ask you questions (cue the red faces).

5) Some or all of these changes might not happen until your child is at secondary school but for a few they can all happen young.

Giving your child a book on puberty could be a good way of allowing them to be curious and get the right information without the embarrassing 'talk'. One example is What's Happening to Me? — there are separate versions for girls and boys.

Health & Wellbeing

Special Educational Needs or Disability

A school's Special Educational Needs or Disability (SEND) system is there to support children who need extra help with their learning. It also looks to help children who have difficulties socialising with others.

What sort of special needs are there?

There are <u>four main categories</u> of special needs:

The website for your child's school should have important information like the school's SEND policy and the local authority's SEND provision (also known as 'the Local Offer'). Schools all follow the government's SEND code of practice which can be found online.

① Developmental

Dyslexia
Difficulty with reading and spelling because words can seem <u>blurred</u> or <u>to move around</u> on a page. Children may also struggle to learn <u>sequences</u> like the days of the week or times tables.

Dyspraxia
Difficulty with <u>fine control</u> like writing or doing up buttons. Children may seem <u>clumsy</u> and <u>bump into things</u>.

Processing disorders
Difficulty in <u>remembering instructions</u> or <u>following a conversation</u>.

Down's Syndrome
A <u>chromosomal disorder</u> which affects a child's <u>ability to learn</u>.

② Behavioural or emotional

Attention Deficit Disorder (ADD)
Children with ADD have a tendency to be <u>easily distracted</u> or <u>struggle to focus</u> on a set task.

Attention Deficit Hyperactivity Disorder (ADHD)
Like ADD, but the hyperactivity may cause children to <u>call out</u> and they may show a <u>lack of self-control</u>.

Autism
Autism affects children in <u>different ways</u> but it's usually linked to difficulties <u>socialising</u>, <u>communicating</u> and dealing with <u>changes to routine</u>. Autistic children often <u>repeat behaviours</u> or <u>words</u>.

Asperger Syndrome
Asperger syndrome is a form of <u>autism</u>. Children with Asperger's can usually communicate as well as their classmates but <u>struggle</u> to <u>join in conversations</u> or pick up on how others may be <u>feeling</u>. Their interests or behaviours may sometimes appear <u>obsessive</u>.

There are several different words used to describe autism and autistic people. To find out more, take a look at the National Autistic Society's website.

③ Sensory

The most common sensory special needs are <u>visual</u> and <u>hearing impairments</u>.

In the past, children with sensory or physical special needs may have been taught in special schools. Nowadays the large majority are taught in mainstream schools with specialised equipment and teaching assistants trained to make their learning more accessible.

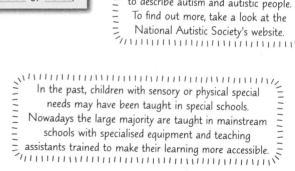

④ Physical

Examples of physical special needs include <u>muscular dystrophy</u>, <u>cerebral palsy</u>, <u>chronic asthma</u> and <u>epilepsy</u>.

Special Educational Needs or Disability

What do I do if I think my child has a special need?

1) If you have <u>concerns</u> that your child is having <u>trouble learning</u> or <u>socialising</u>, talk to the their teacher who will have a sense of whether they are <u>significantly different</u> from their classmates.

2) If after doing this you're <u>still concerned</u> or feel action needs to be taken, <u>ask for a meeting</u> with the school's <u>SEND Co-ordinator</u> (also called SENCo or SENDCo).

Lots of <u>adjustments</u> can be made to help children at school — e.g. <u>coloured overlays</u> for children with dyslexia, sitting children <u>away from distractions</u> or providing <u>common words on a laminated sheet</u> for easy reference. Schools will try strategies like these <u>first</u> as employing extra teaching assistants will have a <u>big impact</u> on the school budget.

What if my child needs extra help?

1) If your child needs help like a <u>dedicated teaching assistant</u> or <u>specialised equipment</u>, an application for an <u>Education, Health and Care Plan (EHCP)</u> may need to be made.

2) These were previously known as '<u>statements</u>'. Applications are usually made by the <u>SENCo</u> but can also be made by <u>a parent or a health care professional</u>.

How does a child get an EHCP?

1) For the EHCP application, both <u>reports</u> and <u>assessments</u> are needed. These may come from <u>child psychologists</u>, <u>paediatricians</u> or <u>other professionals</u> who have worked with the child. There will also be statements from <u>parents</u>, <u>teachers</u> and <u>the child</u>.

2) The local authority is most likely to agree to funding an EHCP if a <u>range of evidence</u> has been gathered. It's important that the school and parents have a <u>close working relationship</u> so they can put forward a <u>strong case</u>.

How long does it take?

- It can take <u>some time</u> to gather all the <u>relevant reports</u> and show that different strategies have been tried and found to be <u>inadequate</u>. For children whose difficulties are less severe, it may take <u>months</u> or even <u>years</u>.

- Once an application for an EHCP has been made, the Local Authority should respond <u>within 16 weeks</u>. If the application is <u>turned down</u> or if the offer is <u>less than you were expecting</u>, you have 28 days to <u>appeal the decision</u>.

For more detailed advice about the help SEND children are entitled to, visit www.gov.uk/ children-with-special- educational-needs

It's not always easy but remember that support is available

Having a child with special needs or a disability (or both) can be challenging. It's important for everyone involved that you have the right support in place. Talk to the school about accessing any help that's available to you.

Phonics — A Parents' Guide

Before we launch into what they'll learn in English, here's a bit of an overview of Phonics. It's the way children are taught to read nowadays, as it gives them the means to decode many new written words.

Phonics is basically matching sounds with letters

For example, the word 'cat' is made up of three sounds: c - a - t.

> The sounds in words are called phonemes.

> The letters used to represent these sounds are called graphemes.

Sometimes one sound is represented by more than one letter.
So in the word 'wish', there are three sounds: w - i - sh.

> When a sound is represented by two letters like this, it's called a digraph.
> If a sound is represented by three letters (e.g. 'igh' in 'night'), it's called a trigraph.

There are also vowel digraphs, such as 'ai' in rain, and also split digraphs (see the next page).

Children start by segmenting and then move on to blending

Segmenting

Children are first taught to segment words — this just means to say the sounds individually.

Children need to segment and blend in order to 'sound words out' when reading and writing them. They might use 'rhythm sticks' to tap out each sound in a word.

> What are the sounds in the word 'crisp'?

> c - r - i - s - p

Diego and Luis knew all about crisp sounds.

Blending

They'll then start blending sounds together to make words.

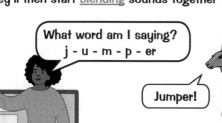

> What word am I saying?
> j - u - m - p - er

> Jumper!

- Ask your child to identify a sound, e.g. of a bird, or car horn, then to copy the sound.
- Sing or say rhymes together. Help your child to spot rhyming words.

HELP AT HOME

Phonics — A Parents' Guide

Children will learn letters and sounds in a set order

Reception

 1. s, a, t, p, i, n, m, d

 2. g, o, c, k, ck, e, u, r, h, b, f, ff, l, ll, ss

 3. j, v, w, x, y, z, zz, qu, ch, sh, th, ng, ai, ee, igh, oa, oo, ar, or, ur, ow, oi, ear, air, ure, er

 4. Words with adjacent consonants, e.g. de**sk**, si**nk**, **thr**ow, **cr**i**sp**

In Reception, children may write words in <u>frames</u> which have one box for <u>each sound</u> in the word, e.g.

y | aw | n

HELP AT HOME

When making consonant sounds, make them really short, without an 'uh' on the end (e.g. 'rrr' not 'ruh'). It's how they'll be taught at school as it helps when they start reading.

Year 1

 1. ay, ou, ie, ea, oy, ir, ue, aw, wh, ph, ew, oe, au, ey

 2. Split digraph (as in 'tape'): a-e, e-e, i-e, o-e, u-e

 3. Alternative pronunciations of graphemes (e.g. st**ea**l, w**ea**lth)

 4. Alternative spellings of phonemes (e.g. b**ear**d, sph**ere**, ch**eer**)

 5. Further practice with words of <u>more than one syllable</u>.

No more 'magic E'

When you were at school, you probably learned about the 'magic E', which turned, e.g. 'mat' into 'mate'. If you talk about the 'magic E' to your child, they probably won't get what you're on about. Nowadays, they refer to <u>split digraphs</u>:

'toe': t-oe

'oe' is a <u>digraph</u> (two letters making one sound)

'tone': t-o-n-e

o_e is a <u>split digraph</u> — it's been split apart by the 'n'.

Words which don't follow the rules are often called tricky words

- Children are taught how to spell these tricky words separately, as they go along.
- Some examples of tricky words are:

> **was** It's tricky because it's pronounced 'woz' not 'waz'.

> **said** It's tricky because it's pronounced 'sed' not 'sade'.

<u>Mnemonics</u> are sometimes used to help children spell tricky words, e.g. '<u>S</u>ally <u>A</u>nn <u>I</u>s <u>D</u>ancing' for <u>said</u>.

That all sounds reesonab... reazonab... wreezunerb... errrr ... fine.

It's not easy to understand phonics from words written on a page, so we've made a short **video** explaining it all dead clearly. You'll find it at www.cgpbooks.co.uk/phonics-help, or use this QR code.

English — Reception

Speaking and listening form a large part of what children will do in English in Reception.
If your child can communicate well before going to school, it'll definitely hold them in good stead.

They'll probably have some sort of story time every day

1) A lot of your child's time in Reception will be spent listening to and talking about stories.

   - The teacher will encourage them to link what they read or hear to their own experiences.

   - Stories might include repeated bits where the children join in, maybe with actions:

   "There's somebody at the door. Who could they be for?"

2) As well as stories, they may also read poems together — such as humorous ones by Michael Rosen.

3) They'll also meet non-fiction texts, which are matched to their interests, or to topics they're learning about, e.g. dinosaurs or space. The teacher may have a 'big book' version so that the whole class can see the features, such as the index.

Learning to Listen

Children will be taught to listen to the teacher and to each other. They'll learn that they shouldn't call out when other people are talking — and that they need to take turns in a conversation.

All of a sudden, they'll be able to read

Yep, just like that, they'll be reading Jane Austen and Shakespeare. Well, perhaps not, but by the end of Reception they might be able to read short stories made up of simple sentences, like the one on the right.

- If your child gets stuck on a word when reading their reading book to you, remind them to sound out the letters, then blend them together. **HELP AT HOME**

- Encourage your child to read words on signs, posters and packaging.

When two letters make one sound, the letters may be underlined. This shows children not to try to sound out the letters individually.

It was just a little seed.

Then there was a green shoot.

Soon it was as big as me.

Now it's as big as my dad.

They'll write some words and short phrases

Your child will learn to do things like write their name on a label, and complete short sentences like:

When we went to the garden, we saw

trees and a berd
....

Children spell lots of words incorrectly when they first start writing. Don't worry about correcting them at this stage — it's more important that they learn to feel comfortable and confident communicating by writing. **HELP AT HOME**

English — Year 1

In Year 1, your child's reading will develop quickly. They'll read words more fluently — i.e. without sounding them out first, and they'll learn more tricky words, meaning they're able to read more interesting sentences.

Your child will be encouraged to discuss what they've read

- During story time, your child might be asked <u>why</u> they think a character does a certain thing.

  Why does the mouse pretend to be the Gruffalo?

  This shows that the child is starting to pick up on <u>inferences</u> from what they're reading.

- They may also make <u>predictions</u> about what will happen next in a story.

Do you have a girlfriend?

Teachers will try to keep children focused on what they're learning and discourage them from blurting out things that are irrelevant.

They'll start using basic punctuation

1) Children will learn to use <u>full stops</u> and <u>capital letters</u> to separate sentences, and to use <u>capital letters</u> for the <u>names of people and places</u>.

2) They'll start to write <u>short recounts</u> about what they did at the weekend:

> On Sunday we went for a walk up a big hill. It was cold. I wore a scarf.

Make sure you write about this at school and not that you went to McDonald's.

Sounds really obvious... but the more time you can spend talking with your child at home, the better they'll progress with English. If they can't say it, they won't be able to write it.

Different schools have different approaches to handwriting

Schools <u>vary</u> in how and when they introduce <u>joined up writing</u>. In Year 1 they may start to join up <u>some</u> letters. ⟶

E.g. diagonal joins: at, th, in
horizontal joins: on, oo, wa

- Encourage your child to hold their pencil correctly so they have more control.
- If your child is left-handed, writing can be extra tricky. It'll help if the page is a little to their left, so they have a good view of the pencil tip. Also, try tilting the page down to the left slightly.

HELP AT HOME

English — Year 2

In Year 2, your child should hopefully be getting increasing enjoyment out of stories and non-fiction books.

Children will start to give opinions about what they read

1) In the stories they read as class, they should be able to give opinions about characters and justify their point of view:

> "I think Gregory is a good character because..."
>
> "I agree with what Gregory did because..."

As their reading develops, they'll be encouraged to add more expression when they read out loud.

2) They may also read some short poems and talk about the particular words and phrases that they like.

- It's good to read longer stories with your child over several sittings, such as *Matilda* by Roald Dahl. This will develop their powers of concentration, and get them more emotionally involved in what you're reading.
- Great stories you might like to read with your child at this age are *The Hodgeheg* by Dick King-Smith, *Gorilla* by Anthony Browne and *The Lighthouse Keeper's Lunch* by David and Ronda Armitage.

HELP AT HOME

TOP TIP:
If your child stumbles over 5 or more words per page when they're reading, the level of their book is probably too high.

If they can read it completely fluently, they may need to read something more challenging if they are to progress, although it's fine if they're reading for pleasure.

They'll have to get to grips with awkward spellings

1) By the end of Year 2, your child should be able to read words with two or more syllables, including lots of tricky words — for example:

> Christmas people
> sugar beautiful

2) They'll be getting to grips with the spellings of some tricky words, but in general they'll be able to read a lot more words than they can correctly spell.

Many children still reverse some letters at this age — it isn't necessarily a sign of dyslexia. Most will soon outgrow it.

Their writing will start to become more complex

1) Your child should start to write more complex sentences, using conjunctions like 'when', 'if', 'that' and 'because'.

Conjunctions are words which link parts of the sentence together. See the Glossary on pages 41-44 for an explanation of the grammatical terms your child may come across.

In terms of punctuation, they'll start to...
- use commas for lists:
> We had chicken, peas, potatoes and gravy.
- use exclamation marks and question marks:
> What an amazing hat! Is it yours?

Writing tasks often link to stories that have been read in the classroom. E.g. after reading Hansel and Gretel, children may be asked to imagine they've been staying in the witch's house, and to write a letter to a friend describing it.

2) They'll be expected to write stories with familiar settings. E.g. they might write about animals in the school playground.

English — Year 3

In Year 3, they'll come across a wide range of texts — including myths and legends.

Children will start to work more independently

1) The teacher might give the children <u>small research tasks</u> to do on their own or in small groups. E.g.

- Children might be asked to use <u>books</u> or the <u>internet</u> to find out the kinds of toys that Victorian children used to play with.
- They'll then <u>explain</u> what they've found, and maybe even answer <u>questions</u> from other children.

2) <u>Drama activities</u>, like '<u>Conscience Alley</u>', may be used to help them explore characters' thoughts and feelings.

They'll improve their writing

By Year 3, children should be fairly comfortable with terms such as <u>verb</u>, <u>noun</u> and <u>adjective</u>.

For definitions of these terms see the Glossary on pages 41-44.

They'll also be encouraged to develop more interesting '<u>noun phrases</u>' in their writing.

E.g. instead of saying: the sky

they could say: the starry sky alive with bats

In terms of punctuation, by now they should be using <u>apostrophes</u> for <u>contractions</u>,

e.g.: <u>It's</u> raining and <u>they're</u> getting wet.

And they'll be taught to use <u>inverted commas</u>*,

e.g.: "Tara wants to go home," she said.

*previously known as speech marks

They'll use a dictionary

We all know you can look up the meaning of words on the <u>internet</u>. But, using a <u>dictionary</u> is good for children — partly because it reinforces their knowledge of the <u>alphabet</u>, and also because they'll tend to discover <u>new interesting words</u> while they're using it.

Conscience Alley

'Conscience Alley' is a popular <u>drama</u> activity used when a character has a <u>dilemma</u>.

One of the children pretends to be the character, and the other children stand on each side giving advice — either for or against a course of action. The child walks down the 'alley' and listens to all the advice.

You should because...
You should NOT because...
It's a GOOD idea to...
It's a BAD idea to...
You may gain...
You may lose...

At the end, the child walking down Conscience Alley will say what they've decided to do.

So that's what that word I'm not allowed to say means!

English — Year 4

By Year 4, children are aware that writers make choices about the language they use — and that these choices have an effect on the reader. They also start to think about the effectiveness of their own writing.

Your child will be expected to be able to use Standard English

1) This isn't about trying to change your child's dialect or accent — it's about making sure that children <u>can</u> use Standard English when they <u>need to</u> in their speech and writing.

2) Here are some examples of Non-Standard vs. Standard English:

Standard English can be spoken in any accent.

I ain't done 'owt. He decked me.

Non-Standard	Standard
"He could of..."	"He could have"
"We done..."	"We did..."
"I didn't see nothing."	"I didn't see anything."
"them shoes"	"those shoes"

HELP AT HOME

It will help your child if you can make them <u>aware</u> of the parts of their dialect which are non-standard. Then they can switch to the standard form when necessary — particularly in their writing.

They learn some poems by heart

1) Your child may <u>learn and perform a short poem</u> — like Christina Rossetti's *Who has seen the wind?*:

Who has seen the wind?
Neither I nor you:
But when the leaves hang trembling,
The wind is passing through.

Who has seen the wind?
Neither you nor I:
But when the trees bow down their heads,
The wind is passing by.

2) The children may then go on to write their <u>own poem</u> that has the same 'question-and-answer' <u>structure</u>.

Hotseating

Hotseating is another common drama activity. One of the children sits in the 'hotseat' and <u>pretends to be a character</u> the class has been learning about. It could be a character from a book, or a famous person they've been studying in History. The child has to <u>answer questions</u> put to them by their classmates.

Rosie loved hotseating but didn't like being asked questions.

They'll vary their sentences with adverbials

Their writing will become more <u>varied</u> and <u>fluent</u>. So they'll progress from something like this:

Chester is on the River Dee in Cheshire. It has a city wall dating back to Roman times. It has a very old racecourse. Lots of people visit Chester.

to something like this:

Chester is on the River Dee in Cheshire. <u>Around the old city</u> is a wall dating back to Roman times. <u>On race days</u>, the city is particularly busy with visitors to the 'Roodee', thought to be the oldest racecourse in the world still in use today.

The underlined bits are called <u>adverbials</u>. They add more information to sentences, and link ideas together.

English — Year 5

By now your child should be getting more confident at expressing their ideas, verbally and in writing.

Your child will be encouraged to justify their opinions

1) Your child will learn to give <u>reasons</u> for their ideas, and develop <u>arguments</u> to support their opinions. They might do this through activities like this one:

I'm wearing these shoes for non-uniform day.

HELP AT HOME

If your child says something you don't agree with, ask them to explain why they have that opinion. They may change their mind when they start to interrogate their own thinking.

Parachute Debate

In this activity, the children each pick a character from a story they've been reading. All the characters are on an <u>imaginary plane</u> which is in trouble — and there's only <u>one parachute</u> on board. They have to <u>persuade the others</u> that their character deserves the parachute.

2) They'll also be expected to give <u>well-structured descriptions</u> and <u>explanations</u>.

> For instance, they might have to <u>explain to the rest of the class</u> how they did a <u>science experiment</u> — e.g. what they did, why they did it, what they learned and what they might do differently next time.

They'll start to learn the key features of different types of texts

1) Your child will learn how to write for <u>different purposes</u>, and what <u>features</u> to include in different types of writing. For example:

Key features of persuasive writing

- <u>Repetition</u> is when certain words or phrases are used more than once.
- A <u>list of three</u> is the use of three words or phrases to describe something.
- <u>Rhetorical questions</u> are questions that don't need an answer.
- <u>Exaggeration</u> is making something sound better or worse than it actually is.

e.g. Pizza scissors are a <u>great</u> product and a <u>great</u> addition to your kitchen.

e.g. Pizza scissors are <u>practical</u>, <u>easy to use</u> and <u>great value</u>.

e.g. Do you want to be able to cut pizza <u>safely and easily</u>?

e.g. Pizza scissors are the <u>best thing you will ever buy</u>.

Children will learn to spot techniques such as <u>metaphors</u> (saying one thing is another) and <u>personification</u> (giving human characteristics to non-human things or events).

The cake was charcoal and her hair was a bird's nest.

2) Your child will practise writing for different purposes, e.g. by making an <u>advertisement</u> for a product, or by writing a <u>letter</u> to their MP asking for more funding for school facilities.

They'll be taught to write with more 'cohesion'

Your child will start to <u>link</u> their sentences and paragraphs so their writing <u>hangs together better</u>.

E.g. | Firstly, ... | In addition, ... | Finally, ... | However, ...

These are all fronted adverbials. See the Glossary on pages 42.

English — Year 6

In Year 6, children get to grips with the idea that language is used differently in different circumstances.

Your child will learn about register

After six years at school your child will be a <u>pro</u> at responding to their name being called out each morning. However, register in English means the <u>type of language</u> which is <u>appropriate for a situation</u>.

1) Your child will learn to <u>vary the register</u> of their own writing.

> Informal language
>> Sayeed, lend us a pencil, can you mate? I've broke mine.
>
> Formal language
>> Please, Mrs Roberts, may I borrow a pencil? I have broken mine.

2) They'll learn features of formal language, such as the use of <u>Standard English</u> and the <u>subjunctive</u> form of a verb.

3) Your child might take part in <u>mock interviews</u> at school to practise speaking in a <u>formal register</u>.

> **HELP AT HOME**
> When watching TV, discuss the register in which people are speaking. E.g. soap opera characters speak differently to MPs in parliament.

> **The Subjunctive**
>
> The subjunctive is a form of a verb which shows that an event is not certain to happen.
>
> E.g. "Your recommendation that the rules <u>be</u> relaxed has been duly considered."
>
> It's often used in <u>subordinate clauses</u> (see the Glossary on page 43).

They'll learn to use loads more punctuation

1) How to write <u>bullet points</u> correctly, e.g.

> Every member of our club should:
> • always wear his or her membership badge.
> • never speak about the club to non-members.
> • use the special handshake.

semi-colon

colon

2) How to use <u>semi-colons</u>, e.g.   Squash is a fast game; bowls is much slower.

...and <u>colons</u> to introduce a <u>list</u>, e.g.   We visited the following cities: Cardiff, Bristol, and Truro.

3) They'll also learn about using <u>hyphens</u> to <u>avoid ambiguity</u>,

e.g.   The boss couldn't read all of the names, so he made everyone resign.

> This should be 're-sign' not 'resign'. (He wasn't that mean.)

They'll use non-fiction texts for research

1) Your child will learn to <u>summarise</u> the <u>main ideas</u> from a text.

2) They might then <u>record the information</u> in a <u>different way</u>, such as in a table.

What's Your Spelling Age?

These multiple-choice questions test the words that the National Curriculum says your child should know how to spell as they move through primary school. The answers are cunningly hidden below...

		A	B	C
Year 1	The .... crept through the night.	thief	theif	thieve
Year 2	The tallest animal at the zoo was the	girafe	giraffe	giraff
Year 2	On Tuesday .... going on holiday to Spain.	their	they're	there
Year 3	I like all food .... pizza.	accept	except	exept
Year 3	It was a .... situation.	humerous	humourous	humorous
Year 4	Someone stole all the .... noses.	snowmen's	snowmens	snowmens'
Year 4	I was very .... for her help.	greatful	grateful	graitful
Year 5	I was glad the hotel could .... us.	accommodate	accomodate	acommodate
Year 6	The .... monkey threw a banana.	mischievious	mischeivous	mischievous
Year 6	I was in a very .... position.	privileged	priviledged	priveleged

Primary English is tricky — that's no ~~exageration~~ ~~eggsageration~~ exaggeration...

The words on the National Curriculum word lists are ones that many adults struggle to spell — I guess that's why they included them. Looking for small words within big words is a strategy children can use to learn the spellings.

Answers: A, B, B, C, A, B, B, C, A, C, A

Spelling, Punctuation & Grammar Glossary

Nowadays children need to be familiar with loads of grammatical terms at primary school.
This glossary will turn you into a Grammar Guru before you can say 'subordinating conjunction'...

Active sentence	A sentence in which the <u>subject</u> does something to the <u>object</u>, e.g. I whacked the fly.
Adjective	A word that describes a noun, e.g. <u>friendly</u> cat, <u>humungous</u> fly.
Adverb	A word that describes a verb, e.g. draw <u>carefully</u>, sing <u>loudly</u>.
Adverbial	A <u>word</u>, <u>phrase</u> or <u>subordinate clause</u> which acts like an <u>adverb</u> — i.e. it describes the verb and gives more context to the sentence. E.g. Brian played basketball <u>after work</u>. I will eat it <u>if it looks nice</u>.
Antonym	A word that means the <u>opposite</u> to another word, e.g. <u>open</u> and <u>closed</u>.
Apostrophe [']	Used to show <u>missing letters</u>, e.g. the dog's shaped like a sausage and <u>belonging</u> (possession), e.g. the dog's sausage.
Article	The words '<u>the</u>', '<u>a</u>' or '<u>an</u>' which go before a noun. A type of <u>determiner</u>.
Brackets [( )]	Used to separate <u>extra information</u> in a sentence.
Capital letter	Used for <u>proper nouns</u> and for <u>starting sentences</u>.
Clause	A bit of a sentence that contains <u>a verb</u> and someone <u>doing the action</u>. E.g. there are two clauses in this sentence: <u>I went to the shops</u> but <u>I didn't buy anything</u>. And one Clause over here.
Colon [:]	Used to introduce some <u>lists</u> and to join <u>sentences</u>.
Comma [,]	Used to separate items in a <u>list</u>, separate <u>extra information</u> and <u>join clauses</u>.
Conjunction	A word or words used to link <u>clauses</u> or <u>words</u> in a sentence, e.g. <u>and</u>, <u>but</u>, <u>since</u>.

Spelling, Punctuation & Grammar Glossary

Contractions		The <u>new word</u> made by <u>joining</u> two words together with an <u>apostrophe</u>, e.g. <u>I'm</u>, <u>he's</u>.
Co-ordinating conjunction		A word that joins two <u>main clauses</u> in a sentence, e.g. <u>and</u>, <u>or</u>.
Dash	—	Used to separate <u>extra information</u> in a sentence or join two <u>main clauses</u> together.
Determiner		A word that goes before a <u>noun</u> to tell you whether it is <u>general</u> or <u>specific</u>. E.g. <u>A</u> cat ate my fish. <u>This</u> cat ate my fish.
Direct speech		The <u>actual</u> words that are <u>said</u> by someone, e.g. "I want to leave," she said.
Exclamation mark	!	Used to show strong <u>feelings</u> and for some <u>commands</u>.
Fronted adverbial		An <u>adverbial</u> at the front of a sentence, separated from the rest of the sentence by a comma, e.g. <u>In spite of the rain</u>, he went for a run.
Full stop		Used to show where a sentence <u>ends</u>.
Homophones		Words that <u>sound the same</u> but have <u>different meanings</u>, e.g. <u>pair</u> and <u>pear</u>.
Hyphen	-	Used to join words or add a prefix.
Inverted commas	" "	Used to show <u>direct speech</u>, e.g. "I'm on my way," shouted the knight.
Main clause		A clause that <u>makes sense</u> on its own, e.g. <u>I water the garden</u> when it is sunny. 'I water the garden' is the main clause.
Noun		A word that <u>names</u> something, e.g. <u>David</u>, <u>scissors</u>, <u>swarm</u>, <u>jealousy</u>.

Spelling, Punctuation & Grammar Glossary

Noun phrase	A group of words which includes a noun and any words that describe it, e.g. Johan opened <u>the heavy old door at the top of the stairs</u>.
Object	The part of the sentence having <u>something done to it</u>.
Parenthesis	Part of a sentence that gives <u>extra information</u>. It is <u>separated</u> from the rest of the sentence by <u>brackets</u>, <u>dashes</u> or <u>commas</u>.
Passive sentence	A sentence in which something is done to the <u>subject</u>, e.g. The window was opened. The apple was eaten.
Phrase	A <u>small part</u> of a sentence, usually <u>without a verb</u>.
Prefix	<u>Letters</u> that can be put <u>in front</u> of a word to change its meaning, e.g. <u>re</u>heat, <u>il</u>legal.
	ill eagle 
Preposition	A word that tells you <u>how</u> things are <u>related</u>, e.g. <u>under</u>, <u>across</u>, <u>during</u>.
Pronoun	A word that can be used <u>instead of a noun</u>, e.g. <u>I</u>, <u>he</u>, <u>we</u>, <u>they</u>.
Question mark	Used at the end of <u>questions</u>.
Reported speech	A <u>description</u> of someone's <u>speech</u>, e.g. She said she needed to leave.
Semi-colon ;	Used to separate <u>lists</u> of longer things and to <u>join</u> sentences.
Subject	The <u>person or thing</u> doing the verb.
Subjunctive form	A verb form that appears in <u>formal</u> writing, e.g. If I <u>were</u> you, I would do it.
Subordinate clause	A <u>less important</u> bit of a sentence which <u>doesn't make sense</u> on its own. E.g. <u>Although I ran it under cold water</u>, my finger still hurt.

Spelling, Punctuation & Grammar Glossary

Subordinating conjunction	A word or group of words which joins a <u>main clause</u> to a <u>subordinate clause</u>, e.g. <u>even though</u>, <u>because</u>.
Suffix	Letters that can be put <u>after</u> a word to change its meaning, e.g. help<u>er</u>.
Synonym	A word with <u>the same</u> or a <u>similar meaning</u> to another word, e.g. <u>happy</u> and <u>cheerful</u>.
Verb	A <u>doing</u> or <u>being</u> word, e.g. you <u>go</u>, it <u>flies</u>, he <u>hops</u>.

Verb forms

Verbs come in a variety of <u>different forms</u> — here are all of the ones they're expected to know...

Simple <u>Past</u> — I **<u>ate</u>**, you **<u>ate</u>**, etc.

Simple <u>Present</u> — I **<u>eat</u>**, you **<u>eat</u>**, etc.

<u>Past</u> Progressive — I **<u>was</u>** eating, you **<u>were</u>** eating, etc.

<u>Present</u> Progressive — I **<u>am</u>** eating, you **<u>are</u>** eating, etc.

<u>Past</u> Perfect — I **<u>had</u>** eaten, you **<u>had</u>** eaten, etc.

<u>Present</u> Perfect — I **<u>have</u>** eaten, you **<u>have</u>** eaten, etc.

Imperative — **Do** your reports! **Tidy** the office, etc.

Subjunctive — If I **were**, I insisted he **go**, etc.

Grammar is back with a vengeance...
You have probably got through life so far without knowing what a subordinating conjunction is, but in recent years, grammar has become a big deal on the English curriculum. Hopefully this glossary has brought you up to speed.

Maths — Reception

Reception might seem like all play, but it's crucial to form a solid foundation before the tricky maths later.

Counting and understanding numbers

- **Say which number is one more or one less than a given number.**
- **Count up to 10 objects — then things you can't touch, like jumps.**
  Don't worry if your child doesn't get this straight away — there's a lot to it, e.g. understanding that the number you assign to the last object is the total number that there are. Also, children have to grasp that the number doesn't change if you switch the order of the objects.
- **Say which group has more objects and which has fewer.**
- **Recognise the written digits up to 10.**
- **Count beyond 20, recognising the pattern.**

"... twenty-_one_, twenty-_two_, twenty-_three_, twenty-_four_..."

- When counting objects, encourage your child to line them up and touch each one while saying the numbers. **HELP AT HOME**
- Read stories with counting, e.g. *The Very Hungry Caterpillar*.
- Sing counting rhymes such as 'Five Currant Buns in a Baker's Shop', or 'Ten in the Bed'. Get your child to act them out, e.g. with teddies.

Ten Frames

Ten frames are often used for helping children visualise numbers.

E.g. **7** can be represented as:

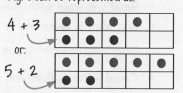

4 + 3

or:

5 + 2

Numicon

Numicon are flat plastic pieces with up to 10 holes in. Children can count the holes, order them from smallest to largest, and even use them for calculating.

3 add 3 makes 6

Adding and subtracting single digits

- **Find the number of objects in two sets by counting.**

"There are 1, 2, 3, 4, 5, 6, 7 apples altogether."

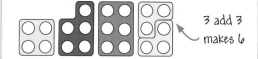

Children will start by counting along a number line with their finger. They'll progress to working mentally, e.g. by "putting the biggest number in their head" and counting on or back.

- **Count on or back to find an answer.**
- **Recall number bonds to 5, and double facts to 10.**

"3 add 2 makes 5."   "4 add 4 makes 8."

- Add Maths to everyday tasks. E.g. there are 3 plates on the table, how many more do we need? **HELP AT HOME**
- Set up a shop where items cost between 1p and 10p. Your child can buy items with pennies, then with 2p and 5p coins.

- **Solve doubling, halving and sharing problems.**

"How many socks are in 5 pairs?"

Making patterns, naming shapes and ordering

- **Recognise and create patterns.**
- **Start to name 2D (flat) and 3D (solid) shapes.**
- **Order up to three objects by length, weight or capacity.**

"The doll is heavier than the teddy."

- **Put familiar events in order, e.g. breakfast, lunch, dinner/tea.**

Show children a variety of patterns, or they can end up thinking that all patterns must be 'ABAB', e.g.

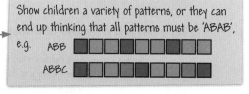

ABB

ABBC

- Connect the names of shapes to objects, e.g. a ball is a sphere.
- Provide pattern-making opportunities, e.g. with leaves and acorns. **HELP AT HOME**

Maths — Year 1

After learning loads in Reception it's time for Year 1. Reading these pages will help you prepare your child so they're ready for the hard work ahead. Luckily there are plenty of fun ways to practise the skills at home.

Getting to know the numbers up to 100

- Count up to 100, both forwards and backwards.
- Read and write each number.
- Say what is one more or less than a number.

  E.g. "Nineteen is one less than twenty."

- Count in twos, fives and tens.

  E.g. "Thirty, thirty-two, thirty-four..."
  "Five, ten, fifteen, twenty..."

Doing this prepares them for starting to learn times tables in Year 2.

 HELP AT HOME
- Encourage your child to count everything — stairs, raisins, lamp posts. Ask your child to guess how many there are first.
- When out and about, spot numbers and read them. E.g. bus numbers and numbers on football shirts.
- Play games involving numbers. E.g. dominoes involves recognising numbers of dots.

Cora had no clue what one less than 20 was, but luckily Sophie seemed to.

Adding and subtracting with numbers up to 20

- Understand simple sums.

  $5 - 2 = 3$ $7 = 4 + 3$

- Work with number bonds up to 20.

  $13 + 7 = 20$ $20 - 7 = 13$

- Solve simple problems.
- Solve missing number problems.

  $10 = 8 + ?$ $7 = ? - 2$

In Year 1, children start by using objects, e.g. cubes, to help them calculate. They'll then progress to using other visual representations.

E.g. Raj has 13 toy cars. He gives 5 to Jill. How many does Raj have left?

This could be modelled using ten frames, or by jumping back along a number line.

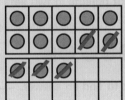

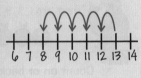

Starting to understand multiplication and division

- Solve simple problems involving sharing and grouping.
- Double numbers and amounts.

  E.g. "Double 7 is 14."

- Find a half and a quarter of a shape or quantity.

 HELP AT HOME
- You can make up number stories at home. E.g. there are six eggs. We use two eggs to bake a cake. How many eggs are left? How do we write the calculation down?
- Encourage your child to share things out equally between friends or family. Instead of them moving around the actual items you could use something else to represent them, e.g. pieces of pasta.

E.g. If the carrots are shared equally between the rabbits, how many carrots does each rabbit get?

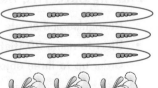

So 12 shared equally between 3 is 4.

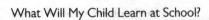

Maths — Year 1

Measuring lots of stuff

- Compare different measurements.

  "Bob is taller than Chung."   "The dog is heavier than the rabbit."

- Use rulers, weighing scales and containers.
- Measure heights, lengths, weights/masses and capacities/volumes.

> **HELP AT HOME**
> - Baking is a great way to get your child measuring and familiar with units of mass and volume.
> - Measure the height of family members and make a height chart.

> Weight and mass are used interchangeably at this stage, even though they have different meanings. It's the same with volume and capacity.

In Year 1, non-standard units are used before standard units.

3 paperclips tall ⟶ 7 cm tall

Understanding time and counting money

- Put events in order.

  "Yesterday was Sunday, today is Monday, tomorrow is Tuesday."
  "Assembly, Maths, playtime, English, lunch."

- Know the days of the week and the months of the year.
- Tell the time when it's on the hour and the half hour.
- Know the values of different coins and notes.

> **HELP AT HOME**
> - Talk to your child about what you're going to do that day using time language. E.g. "First we will have breakfast, then we will get dressed. After that, we'll go to the park."
> - You could talk about what time you'll do each activity and make a timetable.

Recognising shapes

- Name 2D or 'flat' shapes, e.g. rectangles, circles and triangles.
- Name 3D shapes, e.g. cuboids, cubes, pyramids and spheres.

> **HELP AT HOME**
> - Find examples of shapes around the home. E.g. cereal boxes are cuboids, and oranges are spheres.
> - Encourage your child to play with building blocks and other construction toys to help them develop an understanding of shape.

> Shapes can look different depending on which way up they are:
>
> Triangles:
>
>
>
> Squares:

Describing position and movement

- Say where things are in relation to other things.

  "The car is inside the garage."   "The egg is on top of the man's head."

- Describe movement, e.g. up, down, backwards and forwards.
- Recognise whole, half, one-quarter and three-quarter turns.

> A handy way to teach your child to remember left and right is that the left hand makes a capital L. (But you have to remember to look at the back of your hand for it to work.)

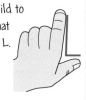

Maths — Year 2

Time flies and before you know it, your child is in their last year of KS1 — which was called Top Infants when I was a kid. Read on to find out the maths they need to get to grips with before the end of this year.

Getting even better acquainted with numbers up to 100

- **Count in twos, threes, fives and in tens, forwards and backwards.**

  E.g. "Three, six, nine, twelve..."
  "One hundred, ninety, eighty..."

- **Know the value of each digit in 2-digit numbers.**

- **Show numbers in different ways.**

  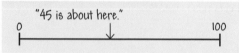
  "45 is about here."

- **Use the more than and less than symbols (< and >).**

  52 > 49   48 < 84

- **Read and write numbers to 100 — in words too.**

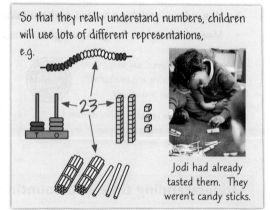

So that they really understand numbers, children will use lots of different representations, e.g.

23

Jodi had already tasted them. They weren't candy sticks.

> **HELP AT HOME**
> Make a 'bead string' of 100 beads where the colour switches after each block of ten. Help your child represent different numbers on it by counting the tens, then the ones.

Adding and subtracting numbers up to 100

- **Use addition and subtraction facts to 20 to work out related facts.**

  5 − 2 = 3   so   50 − 20 = 30

- **Add and subtract two 2-digit numbers and add three 1-digit numbers.**

  45 + 28 = 73   91 − 13 = 78   5 + 7 + 9 = 21

- **Solve problems — sometimes with two steps.**

  "Sam has £14 and he spends £2. His dad gives him £5. How much does he have now?"

- **Know that numbers can be added in any order, but that this doesn't work with subtraction.**

  "16 + 14 is the same as 14 + 16,
  but 16 − 14 is NOT the same as 14 − 16."

- **Solve missing number problems using the 'inverse relationship' between addition and subtracting (the fact that these operations 'undo' each other).**

  9 + ? = 12 ⟶ ? = 12 − 9

Children should be encouraged to use strategies to add or subtract, e.g.

6 + 5 + 4 = 10 + 5 = 15
6 + 4 = 10

32 − 17 = 15

In Year 2, children are introduced to the terms 'sum' (the total), and 'difference' (the result of subtracting one number from another).

The difference between 10 and 11 is not "that one has a circle and the other doesn't".

> **HELP AT HOME**
> - Play a game like snakes and ladders. Ask your child questions such as "How many more are needed to win?"
> - If you've made a 'bead string' as suggested above, hide part of the string in a bag and ask your child to work out how many pieces are hidden.

Maths — Year 2

Learning some times tables

- **Know their 2, 5 and 10 times tables — and the related division facts.**

  $5 \times 7 = 35$ $35 \div 5 = 7$

Each times table fact gives children a 'family' of four facts, e.g. $7 \times 5 = 35$ and $35 \div 7 = 5$ are the other two which complete this family.

- **Know that numbers can be multiplied in any order, but that this doesn't work with division.**

  "2×8 is the same as 8×2 but $8 \div 2$ is NOT the same as $2 \div 8$."

- **Solve problems using multiplication and division.**

  "Pencils are sold in boxes of 10. How many pencils are there in 4 boxes?"

Children can divide by equal sharing or grouping, e.g.

16 treats are shared between 4 dogs. How many treats does each dog get?

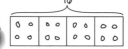

4 doughnuts fit in a box. How many boxes are needed for 16 doughnuts?

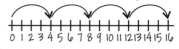

Starting to understand fractions

- **Find simple fractions of a shape or a set of objects.**

  $\frac{3}{4}$ of 20 apples is 15 $\frac{1}{3}$ of the circle is shaded.

- **Know that $\frac{1}{2}$ is the same as $\frac{2}{4}$.**

- There are fun apps for times tables practice. Encourage your child to practise for ten minutes each day. **HELP AT HOME**

- Relate real examples, such as sharing out sweets, to times table facts. E.g. $5 \times 4 = 20$, so 20 shared between 5 is 4.

Using measures, money and time

- **Measure lengths, masses, temperatures and capacities in sensible units.**

  "The classroom is 8 metres long."   "The thermometer reading is 18 °C."

- **Find different coin combinations that add up to the same total.**

- **Solve money problems, including giving change.**

  "Bob buys a pencil for 18p and a rubber for 10p. He pays with two 20p coins. How much change does he get?"

- **Tell the time to the nearest 5 minutes.**

This lesson was doing Megan's hair-do no favours...

This relates to the 5-times table. E.g. when the minute hand points to the 4, it's $4 \times 5 = 20$ minutes past the hour.

Describing shape properties and movement

- **Describe the properties of 2D and 3D shapes.**

  "Cubes have 6 faces, 8 vertices and 12 edges."

- **Say what shapes the faces are on 3D shapes.**

  "The pyramid has a square face and four triangle faces."

- **Describe turns in terms of right angles and quarter, half and three-quarter turns, both clockwise and anticlockwise.**

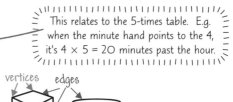
vertices   edges
faces

- Look around at home for boxes of different shapes and count the faces, edges and vertices. Warning: this may lead to increased chocolate consumption.   **HELP AT HOME**

- Download ScratchJr — a free coding app for children aged 5-7. By dragging blocks, your child can programme a character's movements.

Maths — Year 3

It's a giant leap into Key Stage 2, and the first port of call is Year 3. Prepare yourself with these pages.

It's all about numbers up to 1000

- **Read and write each number — with digits and words.**

  981 = nine hundred and eighty-one

- **Understand the value of each digit in 3-digit numbers.**

- **Say what is 10 or 100 more (or less) than a number.**

  "981 is 100 more than 881."
  "981 is 10 less than 991."

- **Count in fours, eights, fifties and hundreds.**

  "8, 16, 24, 32...."
  "50, 100, 150, 200...."

Place Value Grids

These are often used to help children understand the value of each digit in a number.

E.g. **147** can be split into hundreds (H), tens (T) and ones (O) and represented as:

H	T	O

Challenge your child to see what number they can count up to in 15 seconds, counting in fours or eights.

HELP AT HOME

Adding and subtracting using different methods

- **Mentally add or subtract ones, tens or hundreds.**

  254 − 20 = 234   254 + 400 = 654

- **Use column addition and subtraction.**

  $$\begin{array}{r} 2\ 9\ 4 \\ +\ 3\ 8\ 6 \\ \hline 6\ 8\ 0 \\ \end{array}$$

  It's better to talk about 'exchanging', rather than 'carrying the one', or 'borrowing'.

- **Use estimation to check an answer.**

  "294 is near 300, and 386 is near 400.
  So 294 + 386 is about 700."

- **Use addition to check subtractions, and vice-versa.**

  420 − 170 = 250   Check: 250 + 170 = 420

When you're next out shopping, ask your child to work out the total cost of two items that you're buying. You can convert the pounds to pence so they have two 3-digit numbers to work with.

HELP AT HOME

Children should understand what they're doing in column addition and subtraction. 64 + 40 is modelled below:

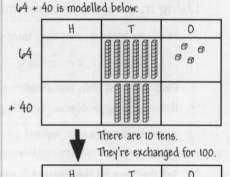

There are 10 tens.
They're exchanged for 100.

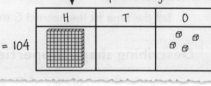

Due to four G&Ts the night before, Miss Lacy decided to swap column addition for a vaguely educational film.

Maths — Year 3

Know and use multiplication facts

- Learn their 3, 4 and 8 times tables.
- Solve multiplication and division problems, including scaling things up and down.

  "The toy bus is 5 times as long as the toy car. The toy car is 9 cm long. How long is the bus?"

- Multiply 2-digit numbers by single digits.

They should already know the 2, 5 and 10 times tables.

Children use informal methods before they use short or long multiplication or division. E.g. 23×4:

T	O
10 10 10	1 1
10 10 10	1 1
10 10 10	1 1
10 10 10	1 1

4 lots of 32
= 12 tens + 8 ones
= 120 + 8 = 128
So $4 \times 32 = 128$

Work with fractions

- **Count up and down in tenths.**
  This prepares children to learn about decimals.
- **Find fractions of a set of objects.**

  $\frac{4}{5}$ of 20 apples is 16.

- **Recognise equivalent fractions.**
- **Simple adding and subtracting.**

  $\frac{1}{5} + \frac{2}{5} = \frac{3}{5}$ $\frac{7}{8} - \frac{1}{8} = \frac{6}{8}$

Bar models are great for comparing fractions. The one below shows that $\frac{1}{3} = \frac{2}{6}$, and that $\frac{1}{5}$ is bigger than $\frac{1}{6}$.

$\frac{1}{5}$	$\frac{1}{5}$	$\frac{1}{5}$	$\frac{1}{5}$	$\frac{1}{5}$
$\frac{1}{6}$	$\frac{1}{6}$	$\frac{1}{6}$	$\frac{1}{6}$	$\frac{1}{6}$	$\frac{1}{6}$
$\frac{1}{3}$		$\frac{1}{3}$		$\frac{1}{3}$	

Can I have three-sixths of your sweets?

No. Three-quarters. Take it or leave it.

Meany.

Work with measures, money, time and angles

- **Measure using a range of units.**

  "200 cm = 2 m"   "It's better to weigh elephants in kilograms than grams."

- **Measure the perimeter (distance around the edge) of shapes.**
- **Add money in pounds and pence, and work out the amount of change.**

  "£2.48 + 72p = £3.20. If I pay with £5, I'll get £5 – £3.20 = £1.80 change."

- Tell the time to the nearest minute — even on clocks with Roman numerals.
- Identify right angles in shapes, and use them to describe turns.

Help your child to find the masses on food packaging, e.g. on butter and flour. Talk about the units they're given in.

HELP AT HOME

Right angles are marked with little squares, e.g.

Use charts and tables

- Make bar charts, pictograms and tables to show data.
- Use graphs with scales.

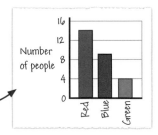

Ask your child to count how many sweets of each colour or type there are in a packet and make a tally chart of the data. Then get them to display the data on a bar chart or pictogram.

HELP AT HOME

Maths — Year 4

Onwards and upwards into Year 4. Bigger numbers, more methods, and the dreaded decimals.

Understanding numbers with four digits

- Understand the value of the digits in 4-digit numbers.
- Say what is 1000 more or less than a number.

  "7657 is 1000 more than 6657."

- Count in steps of 6, 7, 9, 25 and 1000.

  "7, 14, 21, 28..."   *"25, 50, 75, 100..."*

- Round numbers to the nearest 10, 100 or 1000.

  "7657 is 7660 to the nearest 10, 7700 to the nearest 100 and 8000 to the nearest 1000."

- Read Roman numerals to 100.
- Count backwards through zero.

  E.g. in tens from 18: "18, 8, −2, −12 , −22..."

> There's a great pattern in the multiples of 9 — the digits in each one add up to 9.
> E.g. **27** = 2 + 7 = 9, **54** = 5 + 4 = 9.

HELP AT HOME

- Help your child learn their times tables by saying them out loud — your child should join in as much as they can.
- Play board games that involve addition, e.g. Scrabble and Monopoly.
- Look out for Roman numerals, e.g. Henry VIII, and also negative numbers, e.g. a temperature of −3 °C.

Adding and subtracting bigger numbers

- Add and subtract 4-digit numbers using formal column methods — see page 50.
- Use mental methods to add and subtract.

  E.g. the compensation strategy: 297 + 651
  +3↓ −3↓
  300 + 648 = 948

- Solve two-step problems.

Bar models can help children understand word problems.
E.g. Zane has 160 cards and Shaheen has 100. Zane gives 40 cards to Shaheen. How many more cards than Zane does Shaheen now have?

A baa model

Draw a bar model with the known information:

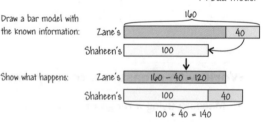

Zane's: 160 ... 40
Shaheen's: 100

Show what happens:
Zane's: 160 − 40 = 120
Shaheen's: 100 ... 40
100 + 40 = 140

Shaheen has 140 − 120 = **20 more cards than Zane**.

Multiplying and dividing bigger numbers mentally

- Know all their times tables — all the way up to 12 × 12.
- Multiply and divide bigger numbers using times table facts.

  30 × 4 = 120   200 ÷ 5 = 40

- Multiply by zero — this always gives zero.
- Use factor pairs in mental calculations.
- Solve trickier problems using multiplication and division.

  "Plant pots contain 3 blue flowers and 5 red flowers. I have 20 red flowers. How many blue flowers do I have?"
  20 ÷ 5 = 4 pots. There are 3 blue flowers in each pot so I have 4 × 3 = 12 blue flowers.

Factor pairs are pairs of numbers which multiply to give a certain number, e.g. the factor pairs of 16 are 2 × 8 and 4 × 4.

Here's how you use them in mental maths:

16 × 5

Multiplying by 16 is hard, so replace it with 2 × 8. (2 × 8) × 5

Swap the order around. 2 × 5 × 8
= 10 × 8 = 80

Maths — Year 4

Use more than one type of written multiplication and division

- Use short multiplication and division (with no remainders).

$$\begin{array}{r} 6\ 4\ 7 \\ \times\ \ \ \ \ 6 \\ \hline 3\ 8\ 8\ 2 \\ \tiny 2\ 4 \end{array}$$

4) 6 ^{2}9 ^{1}2 = 1 7 3

This is sometimes called the 'bus stop' method.

- Use the 'grid' or 'box' method to multiply 2-digits by 1-digit.

The **grid method** involves breaking numbers up into parts and multiplying each part separately.
E.g.
24 × 7

×	20	4
7	140	28	= 168

Add these to get the answer.

Use fractions and make sense of decimals

- Write tenths and hundredths as decimals.
- Divide by 10 and 100 to end up with a decimal number.

$$14 \div 10 = 1.4 \qquad 14 \div 100 = 0.14$$

- Know equivalent fraction 'families', e.g. $\frac{1}{4} = \frac{2}{8} = \frac{3}{12}$
- Find fractions where the top number (numerator) isn't 1.

$$\frac{1}{5} \text{ of } 20 = 4, \text{ so } \frac{3}{5} \text{ of } 20 = 3 \times 4 = 12$$

- Adding and subtracting of fractions.

$$\frac{1}{5} + \frac{3}{5} = \frac{4}{5} \qquad \frac{4}{7} - \frac{1}{7} = \frac{3}{7}$$

Grids are often used to show tenths and hundredths. The whole grid is one whole.

 $\frac{7}{10} = 0.7$ $\frac{32}{100} = 0.32$

Decimals can also be shown on place value charts. E.g. 0.14:

Tens	Ones	Tenths	Hundredths
	●	●	●●●●

These are good for showing division by 10 or 100. You move the counters 1 place right to divide by 10, and 2 places right to divide by 100.

Converting measures and finding perimeters

- Convert between different units.

1 km = 1000 m, 1 m = 100 cm, 1 hour = 60 minutes

- Find perimeters and count squares to find areas.
- Use the 24-hour clock.

Involve your child in solving real life problems. E.g. Wallpaper is 53 cm wide. How many strips are needed for a 4 m wide wall?

HELP AT HOME

Perimeter is the distance around a shape. Side lengths may have to be worked out:

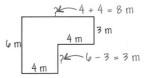

4 + 4 = 8 m
3 m
6 m
4 m
6 − 3 = 3 m
4 m

Perimeter = 6 + 8 + 3 + 4 + 3 + 4
= 28 m

Plot graphs and coordinates

- Use simple coordinates.
- Describe 'translations' (sliding movements) from one point on a grid to another.
- Draw bar charts and graphs to show stuff changing over time.

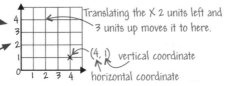

Translating the X 2 units left and 3 units up moves it to here.

(4, 1) vertical coordinate
horizontal coordinate

Marcus's coordinates plotted something really rude.

Maths — Year 5

Year 5 — the start of upper Key Stage 2. It's time for prime numbers, cube numbers and obtuse angles.

Understanding numbers up to at least one million

- **Read, write and compare numbers to at least 1 000 000.**
- **Rounding up numbers.**

  "455 600 is 460 000 to the nearest 10 000."

- **Read Roman numerals to 1000.**

  MDL = 1550 (M = 1000, D= 500, L = 50)

- **Understand negative numbers (e.g. temperatures).**
- **Describe sequences involving fractions and decimals.**

  Add $\frac{1}{4}$ each time: ...5, $5\frac{1}{4}$, $5\frac{1}{2}$, $5\frac{3}{4}$, 6, $6\frac{1}{4}$ ..."

Reading and writing big numbers is tricky when zeros are involved. E.g. five hundred and seven thousand and five is 507 005.

THOUSANDS					
HTh	TTh	Th	H	T	O
5	0	7	0	0	5

The zeros are place holders. Without them the number would be 575. Completely wrong.

Numbers like $5\frac{3}{4}$ and $6\frac{1}{4}$ are called a 'mixed numbers'.

Calculating with big numbers

- **Add and subtract big numbers using mental and column methods.**
- **Use long multiplication.**
- **Use short division and understand remainders.**

  6 eggs fit in a box. 327 eggs need to be packed. How many boxes are needed?

  $327 \div 6$ 5 4 r 3
  $6 \overline{)3\ ^3 2\ ^2 7}$

  With 54 boxes, 3 eggs won't fit, so 55 boxes are needed.

  Alternative solution

$$\begin{array}{r} 2\ 7\ 9\ 5 \\ \times\qquad 4\ 3 \\ \hline 8\ 3\ 8\ 5 \\ {}_2\ {}_2\ {}_1 \\ 1\ 1\ 1\ 8\ 0\ 0 \\ {}_3\ {}_3\ {}_2 \\ \hline 1\ 2\ 0\ 1\ 8\ 5 \\ {}_1\ {}_1 \end{array}$$

This is 2795 × 3.
Put a zero here because this is 2795 × 40.
Add products together to get the final answer.

- **Multiply and divide numbers by 10, 100 and 1000.**
- **Solve problems involving any operations and several steps.**

Encourage your child to check answers to calculations are sensible. E.g. to check 2795 × 43 = 120 185, round the numbers to 3000 and 40. 3000 × 40 = 120 000, so the answer is likely to be right.

HELP AT HOME

Gattegno charts are used to help children understand place value and that multiplication and division are inverses.

They might look complicated, but each number is just <u>ten times the number below</u>.

100	200	300	400	500	Each number
10	20	30	40	50	is also the
1	2	3	4	5	number
0.1	0.2	0.3	0.4	0.5	<u>above it</u>
0.01	0.02	0.03	0.04	0.05	<u>divided by 10</u>.

Special types of number

- **Find common multiples of two numbers.**

  12 is a common multiple of 3 and 4.

- **Know what prime numbers are.**
- **Use square and cube numbers.**

  $4^2 = 4 \times 4 = 16$, so 16 is a **square** number.
  $2^3 = 2 \times 2 \times 2 = 8$, so 8 is a **cube** number.

A prime number divides exactly by two numbers, 1 and itself. E.g. 2, 3, 5, 7, 9, 13... (1 only divides exactly by one number, so it isn't prime.)

Maths — Year 5

Percentages (and more fractions and decimals)

- Add fractions with different denominators (bottom numbers).
- Multiply fractions by whole numbers.
- Convert between improper fractions and mixed numbers.

$$\frac{12}{5} = 2\frac{2}{5}$$ twelve fifths = 2 ones and two-fifths

- Write decimal numbers as fractions.

$$0.27 = \frac{27}{100} \qquad 0.027 = \frac{27}{10000}$$

- Solve problems involving numbers with three decimal places.
- Know that per cent means 'parts per 100', and write the percentage and decimal equivalents of simple fractions.

$$\frac{1}{2} = 50\% = 0.5 \qquad \frac{4}{5} = 80\% = 0.8 \qquad \frac{4}{25} = 16\% = 0.16$$

E.g. $\frac{4}{5} + \frac{3}{10}$

In this sum, change $\frac{4}{5}$ to an equivalent fraction with 10 at the bottom. Do the same to both top and bottom:

$$\frac{4}{5} = \frac{8}{10} \quad (\times 2)$$

So $\frac{4}{5} + \frac{3}{10} = \frac{8}{10} + \frac{3}{10} = \frac{11}{10} = 1\frac{1}{10}$

When decimals are added or subtracted, the decimal points need to be lined up. E.g. 18.95 + 6.2:

Line up
```
  1 8 . 9 5
+    6 . 2 0
  2 5 . 1 5
     1 1
```

Filling the gaps with zeros helps keep everything lined up.

Measures and angles

- **Convert between metric and imperial measures.**
  E.g. cm to inches, kg to pounds.
- **Estimate volume and capacity.**
  E.g. by filling a box with centimetre cubes.
- **Calculate perimeters and the areas of rectangles.**
- **Measure and draw angles accurately.**
- **Recognise different types of angles.**

  Acute / Obtuse / Reflex

- **Know some angles rules.**

 Angles around a point add to 360°. / Angles on a straight line add to 180°.

 HELP AT HOME

Ask your child to estimate the volume of a liquid and then to measure it using a measuring jug. You could ask them questions such as, what fraction of a pint does a mug hold? What is it in millilitres?

Algebra may rear its head in area and perimeter calculations. E.g.

The area of this rectangle is 12 m². Find a.

a m, 4 m

Area = length × width
$$= 4 \times a = 12 \rightarrow 4a = 12$$
$$\rightarrow a = 12 \div 4 = 3$$

A cute child / An obtuse child

A few other bits and bobs

- **Tell the difference between regular polygons** (all sides and angles the same, e.g. square) **and irregular polygons** (not all sides or angles the same, e.g. kite).
- **Interpret line graphs and timetables.**

When using public transport get your child to help with the journey times. You can get them to work out the duration of the journey, when you'll arrive, etc. HELP AT HOME

Maths — Year 6

It hardly seems five minutes ago that they were getting to grips with numbers that add together to make 10. Now it's numbers to 10 million, not to mention ratios and algebra. Eeek.

Dealing with numbers up to ten million

- Read, write, round and compare numbers up to 10 000 000.
- Work out the difference between a positive and a negative number.

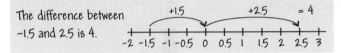

The difference between −1.5 and 2.5 is 4.

Writing numbers in words — definitely the most tedious part of KS2 Maths.

> **HELP AT HOME**
> - With many maths topics, a diagram (e.g. a bar model) makes things clearer. So if your child gets stuck with their homework, suggesting they draw one just might give them the breakthrough they need.
> - Talk positively about maths and encourage perseverance (even if you hated it at school).

More calculating with big numbers

- More adding, subtracting, multiplying and dividing big numbers using mental and written methods.
- Use long division and convert the remainder to a fraction.
- Follow the order of operations when doing calculations.

  Brackets first, then × and ÷, then + and −.

  $1 + 18 ÷ (5 + 4) = 1 + 18 ÷ 9$ (brackets worked out)
  $= 1 + 2 = 3$ (division done before addition)

- Find common factors, common multiples and prime numbers (see page 54).

  Factors of 9 = 1, 3, 9. Factors of 12 = 1, 2, 3, 4, 6, 12.
  Common factors of 9 and 12 = 1, 3

A <u>factor</u> is a number that divides exactly into another number.

E.g. 717 ÷ 12:

```
        5 9
  12 | 7 1 7
     - 6 0 0  ← 12 × 50
       1 1 7
     - 1 0 8  ← 12 × 9
           9  ← remainder
```

As a fraction the remainder is $\frac{9}{12}$
Simplify it by dividing the top and bottom by the highest common factor:

$$\frac{9}{12} = \frac{3}{4} \quad \text{So answer} = 59\frac{3}{4}$$

(÷ 3 top and bottom)

Getting really familiar with fractions and decimals

- Simplify fractions (write the equivalent fraction with the smallest numbers).
- Make fractions all have the same bottom number.
- Multiply fractions and divide them by whole numbers.

This is the key to ordering fractions, and adding and subtracting them.

$\frac{4}{5} × \frac{1}{7} = \frac{4}{35}$ → Multiply top numbers and bottom numbers.

$\frac{4}{5} ÷ 3 = \frac{1}{3} × \frac{4}{5} = \frac{4}{15}$ → Dividing $\frac{4}{5}$ by 3 is the same as finding $\frac{1}{3}$ of $\frac{4}{5}$.

- Know the line in the middle of a fraction works as a division sign.

  $\frac{4}{5} = 4 ÷ 5 = 0.8$

- Do long divisions which give a decimal answer.
- Multiply decimals by whole numbers using short or long multiplication.

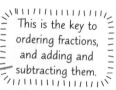

A dab hand at all operations, you say?

Maths — Year 6

Learning to use ratio and proportion

- Solve ratio and proportion problems.

  "There are 63 children in Year 6 and for every 4 girls there are 3 boys. How many girls are there?"

  Draw a bar model:

  63

G	G	G	G	B	B	B

  There are 7 parts. Each part is worth 63 ÷ 7 = 9. No. of girls = 4 × 9 = 36

- Calculate percentages.

  "Find 40% of 150." 10% of 150 is 150 ÷ 10 = 15. So 40% is 4 × 15 = 60.

- Enlarge shapes by scale factors. E.g. scale factor 2 means the side lengths are doubled.

- Help your child make a certain number of pancakes. For 3 pancakes you need 1 egg, 35 g flour, 50 ml milk and 12 g melted butter. For extra pancakes, they'll need to increase the ingredients, keeping them in the same proportions. **HELP AT HOME**

- Work out the approximate scale factor of toys. E.g. if a plastic T-rex is 10 cm tall and a real one was about 5 m tall, the scale factor is 50.

Wow! The ratio of fat and sugar to fruit is perfect.

Using letters in place of numbers — it's got to be algebra

- Use simple formulae.

  "Bags of compost cost £4 each, plus £2.99 delivery." The cost of y bags in pounds is 4y + 2.99.

- Find pairs of numbers that make an equation true.

  If a and b are positive whole numbers, find the pairs of values which make this equation true: $4a + b = 15$

  When $a = 1$, $(4 \times 1) + b = 15$, so $b = 11$
  When $a = 2$, $(4 \times 2) + b = 15$, so $b = 7$
  When $a = 3$, $(4 \times 3) + b = 15$, so $b = 3$
  a can't be 4 or more because $4a = 16$, which is bigger than 15.

  $4a$ means $4 \times a$.

More on measures

- Solve problems involving converting between units. E.g. between miles and kilometres.
- Calculate the area of parallelograms and triangles.

Help your child to map a journey using an app. Get them to convert the distance from miles to km. **HELP AT HOME**

Shapes, angles and coordinate grids

- Make nets that can be folded up into 3D shapes.
- Use angle rules and name parts of a circle.
- Plot coordinates with negative numbers. E.g. (−3, −5).

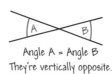

Angle A = Angle B
They're vertically opposite.

circumference
diameter
radius

Sir Cumference

And finally, statistics

- Interpret and draw line graphs and pie charts.
- Work out the mean (average).

  "The number of coffees Pam has each day for 5 days is 4, 4, 5, 7 and 10." The total number was 30, so the mean is 30 ÷ 5 = 6.

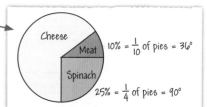

Cheese
Meat
Spinach
$10\% = \frac{1}{10}$ of pies = 36°
$25\% = \frac{1}{4}$ of pies = 90°

What did zero say to eight? Nice belt...

Help your child see how Maths can be useful in real life through things like baking and sale shopping. You can even involve Maths in making decorations — find 3D shape nets online, print them out and stick them together. Voilà!

Science

Before your child learns about the Higgs boson particle, there are a few basics they have to get out of the way. A lot of them are to do with observing the world around them, so they'll need to keep their eyes peeled.

Reception, Year 1 & Year 2

In your child's first years of primary school, Science focuses on the natural and man-made world around them, and they begin to use simple scientific language to talk about what they've learned. They'll:

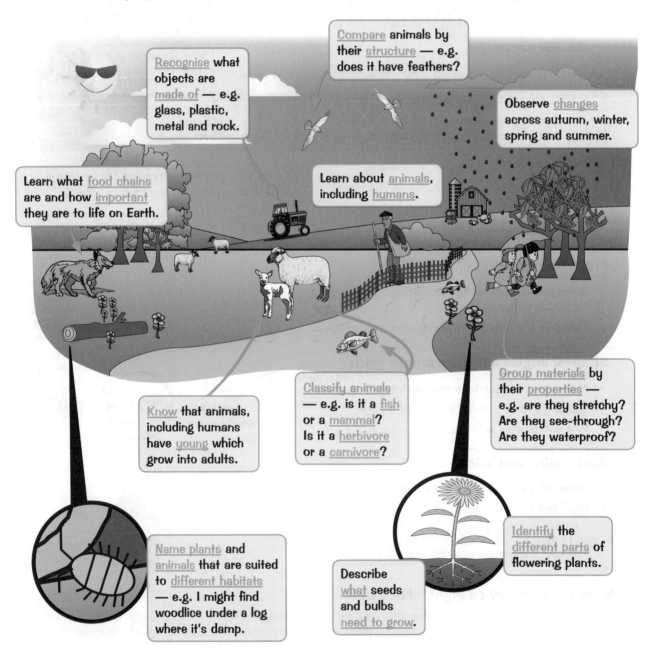

Compare animals by their structure — e.g. does it have feathers?

Recognise what objects are made of — e.g. glass, plastic, metal and rock.

Observe changes across autumn, winter, spring and summer.

Learn what food chains are and how important they are to life on Earth.

Learn about animals, including humans.

Know that animals, including humans have young which grow into adults.

Classify animals — e.g. is it a fish or a mammal? Is it a herbivore or a carnivore?

Group materials by their properties — e.g. are they stretchy? Are they see-through? Are they waterproof?

Name plants and animals that are suited to different habitats — e.g. I might find woodlice under a log where it's damp.

Describe what seeds and bulbs need to grow.

Identify the different parts of flowering plants.

Science

Learning Science at school

A classic activity is for children to <u>plant seeds</u> and <u>observe</u> how they <u>grow into mature plants</u>. They'll be encouraged to think of questions to ask about <u>what is happening</u> and maybe even set up a <u>test</u> to show that plants need water and light to grow well.

Schools often use <u>stories</u> as a <u>context</u> for learning Science. For example, after reading the story of *The Three Little Pigs*, the children might build structures out of a range of materials and investigate which blow down most easily.

How to help your child with Science

Look at the <u>night sky</u> together and talk about <u>what can be seen</u>.

Point out things such as <u>rainbows</u>, <u>lightning</u> and <u>fog</u> to your child.

If you have a <u>pet</u>, get your child involved in looking after it so they <u>understand</u> what it <u>eats</u> and the <u>exercise it needs</u>.

Explore <u>floating</u> and <u>sinking</u> at bath time. Predict whether <u>objects</u> such as a <u>rubber duck</u> or a <u>bar of soap</u> will float, then test them.

<u>Visit</u> an aquarium, a farm, a zoo or even a pet shop and spend time looking and talking about the animals and their <u>differences</u>.

When out walking, talk about how the <u>trees</u> and the <u>leaves</u> change through the year.

<u>Hunt for bugs</u> in the garden or when out on a walk together. Talk about <u>why</u> they live <u>where</u> they live and how different animals need <u>different environments</u>.

<u>Watch</u> wildlife and science programmes together. You can find ones aimed at children, such as <u>Nina and the Neurons</u> and <u>Maddie Moate's</u> videos.

Do some <u>gardening</u> together and grow flowers and food from seeds. Discuss what the plants will <u>need</u> to grow well.

<u>Borrow science books</u> from your local library that interest your child. <u>Read</u> them together at bedtime.

I had a eureka moment but then I forgot what the original point was...

You don't have to go on expensive trips to find out about Science. Hunt through your recycling bin and decide what materials the items are made of, or search for mini-beasts and signs of larger animals in your local park.

Science

Years 3 & 4

Key Stage 2 kicks off by revisiting the Plants and Animals topics that children met in previous years, but in much greater depth. Exciting topics such as electricity and magnetism are also introduced, not to mention super-sciency equipment, like data loggers.

Children will learn:

How plants work

- **The job of <u>each part</u> of the plant — e.g. flowers are essential for <u>pollination</u>, <u>seed formation</u> and <u>dispersal</u>.**

- **What plants <u>need</u> to grow.**

- **How water is <u>transported</u> in plants — e.g. by standing white carnations in coloured water.**

> The children will start to design fair tests (where only one variable is changed at a time). E.g. when testing if plants need light, you must keep the temperature and the amount of water, etc. the same.

HELP AT HOME
Help your child to plant seeds in containers and decide where best in the house to keep them. Try cress or marigolds for quick results.

Forces and magnets

- **How things <u>move</u> differently on different surfaces.**

- **How magnets can <u>attract</u> or <u>repel</u> each other, and how they attract some <u>other materials</u>.**

> Your child will be encouraged to make predictions based on what they already know — e.g. a toy car will move quickly over a smooth surface because it's easy to slide on (a bit like ice).

HELP AT HOME
Encourage your child to experiment with a fridge magnet — which household objects does it stick to?

States of matter

- **How things can be a <u>solid</u>, a <u>liquid</u> or a <u>gas</u>.**

- **How materials <u>change state</u> when heated or cooled.**

- **How condensation and evaporation are involved in the <u>water cycle</u>.**

- Point out examples of condensation to your child. E.g. bathroom mirrors get misty when steam in the air turns back into water on the cooler surface.

- Make rice crispy cakes with your child. This involves chocolate changing state when it's heated, then changing back again when it cools. You could also freeze fruit juice to make ice lollies.

HELP AT HOME

Rocks

- **That rocks can be grouped in <u>different ways</u>.**

- **How <u>fossils are formed</u>.**

- **That soil is made from <u>rock</u> and <u>organic matter</u>.**

> E.g. children might use a lens to see if rocks contain crystals or grains, or they might drop water onto the rocks to test their permeability.

Create salt-dough fossils with your child using a recipe from the internet.
HELP AT HOME

Science

How light behaves

- **That light allows us to <u>see</u> and is <u>reflected from surfaces</u>.**
- **That sunlight can <u>damage eyes</u>.**
- **How <u>shadows form</u> and what causes them to <u>change size</u>.**

- With your child, mark the position of an object's shadow each hour. Link its change to the movement of the Sun.
- Help your child make shadow puppets. What happens to the shadows when you move the torch closer to them?

HELP AT HOME

How sound is produced

- **That sounds are made by <u>vibrations</u> which travel <u>though materials</u>.**
- **How <u>pitch</u> and <u>volume</u> are related to the <u>source</u> and <u>size</u> of the vibrations.**

Help your child make a string telephone using two disposable cups. Experiment with it around the house and outside.

HELP AT HOME

Living things

- **How <u>living things</u> can be grouped in <u>different ways</u>.**
- **How living things can be threatened by <u>environmental changes</u>.**
- **What <u>food chains</u> show.**

Animals (including humans)

- **That animals need <u>food</u> of <u>certain types</u>.**
- **Why some animals need a <u>skeleton</u> and <u>muscles</u>.**
- **The function of each part of the <u>digestive system</u>.**
- **The jobs of the different types of human <u>teeth</u>.**

Give your child the opportunity to plan some of their meals, making sure they include things from each food group.

HELP AT HOME

Electricity and circuits

- **How to make <u>simple circuits</u> using <u>cells</u>, <u>wires</u>, <u>switches</u> and <u>bulbs</u>.**
- **That a bulb only <u>lights</u> when it is part of a <u>complete closed circuit</u>.**
- **That some materials, such as metals, are <u>conductors</u>, whereas others, such as wood and plastic, are <u>insulators</u>.**

Hopefully this time the circuit wouldn't blow...

Solids, liquids and gases — three for the price of one...

Water is a handy substance as it freezes and boils at convenient temperatures. Stick it in the freezer and you make solid ice. Boil it and you get a gas (steam or water vapour). Pretty cool for just plain H_2O.

Science

Years 5 & 6

Now that your child is older, they'll be given the chance to help design their own experiments — deciding what to test, what to observe and how to present their findings. Alongside this they'll learn about:

Living things and their habitats

- The <u>life cycles</u> of plants and different types of animals.

- <u>Reproduction</u> in plants and animals. E.g. a <u>sperm</u> and <u>egg</u> fuse to <u>create offspring</u>. The details of what your child will learn about reproduction <u>beyond the basic science</u> (see page 28) will be set out in the <u>school's sex education policy</u>.

- <u>Classifying living things</u>, including micro-organisms, according to their <u>similarities</u> and <u>differences</u>. E.g. are they vertebrates or invertebrates?

- Go mini-beast hunting with your child in your garden or a park. Identify the creatures you find using the internet or library books, and classify them as arthropods, molluscs or annelids.

- Buy a butterfly habitat and some caterpillars so your child can observe their life cycle at home.

HELP AT HOME

Your child might learn about Carl Linnaeus, a Swedish scientist who created the system for classifying living things that we use today.

Animals (including humans)

- The parts of the <u>human circulatory system</u>, including the roles of the <u>heart</u>, <u>blood vessels</u> and <u>blood</u>.

- The <u>changes</u> humans go through to get to <u>old age</u> — including <u>puberty</u>.

- How <u>diet</u>, <u>exercise</u>, <u>drugs</u> and <u>lifestyle</u> affect how their body works.

- How nutrients and water are <u>transported</u> in animals.

Your child will also learn about puberty in Sex Education (p.28). These changes will hopefully be covered before your child experiences them, so they're armed with the correct information.

Electricity

- How to create <u>electrical circuits</u> using different electrical components.

- <u>Circuit symbols</u> and how to use them in circuit <u>diagrams</u>.

Using an electronics kit, your child will get to <u>experiment</u> with <u>different components</u>, such as <u>switches</u>, <u>bulbs</u> and <u>motors</u>. They might even get to create a useful circuit, e.g. for a burglar alarm.

Evolution and inheritance

- How <u>living things</u> have changed over <u>millions of years</u>.

- How offspring are <u>similar but</u> <u>not identical</u> to their parents.

- How animals and plants are <u>adapted</u> to their <u>environment</u>. E.g. camels are well suited to the desert as their big flat feet stop them sinking in the sand.

These don't look like the Great Pyramids...

Science

Properties and changes of materials

- Grouping <u>materials</u> based on their <u>properties</u> — e.g. do they <u>conduct electricity</u>? Do they <u>dissolve in water</u>? Are they <u>magnetic</u>?

- <u>Uses</u> of metals, wood and plastic, and reasons <u>why</u> they're <u>used</u> for these things, based on <u>evidence</u> from <u>experiments</u>.

- How some things <u>dissolve</u> to form <u>solutions</u>.

- <u>Separating mixtures</u> (e.g. salt and water) using <u>filters</u>, <u>sieves</u> and <u>evaporation</u>.

- <u>Reversible</u> and <u>irreversible</u> changes.

Selecting the right equipment is an important scientific skill.

Your child will use their knowledge of fair testing to create experiments to investigate predications they make. E.g. does the temperature of water affect how easily sugar dissolves?

HELP AT HOME

Baking with your child is a great way to show reversible and irreversible changes — e.g. melting chocolate (reversible) or the action of a raising agent (irreversible).

Light

- How <u>light travels</u> in straight lines and that this means <u>shadows</u> are the <u>same shape</u> as the objects that cast them.

- How we <u>see objects</u> because <u>light reflects</u> off them into our eyes.

Light - - - ▷ ⚹ ⟵ Mirror

Periscopes show that light travels in straight lines.

Forces

- <u>Gravity</u>, <u>air resistance</u>, <u>water resistance</u> and <u>friction</u>.

- <u>Levers</u>, <u>pulleys</u> and <u>gears</u> and how they <u>increase</u> the effect of a <u>small force</u>.

Children may learn about how <u>Galileo</u> and <u>Newton</u> developed the <u>theory of gravity</u>.

Children could be asked to <u>design a pulley system</u> — e.g. using an empty thread spool with a pencil through it. They might work in teams and see which team's design can <u>support</u> the <u>biggest weight</u>.

Earth and space

- The <u>movement</u> of the planets in our <u>solar system</u>.

- The <u>movement</u> of the <u>moon</u> around the <u>Earth</u>.

- What causes <u>day</u> and <u>night</u>.

- Use stargazing apps (e.g. SkyView® Lite or Star Walk Kids) to identify objects in the night sky with your child.

- Help your child track the phases of the moon over a month.

HELP AT HOME

Amelia loved her new telescope, even if she had to draw the planets herself...

Fly like a butterfly, hop like a frog... Wait, what?

You can find loads of at-home Science experiments on the internet. Looking up a few and having a go with your child is a great way for you both to get excited about Science outside of school using readily-available materials.

Art and Design

As well as having the chance to be creative, your child will be taught how art, craft and design are important to the history and culture of where they live. Time to practise those smiles for when artwork comes home...

Reception, Year 1 & Year 2

In Art and Design your child will get the opportunity to let their imagination run free. They'll use different art materials and tools such as paints, pastels, clay, paintbrushes and scissors.

Your child might:

Design and make things from a choice of materials such as Play-Doh®, Lego® or recycled materials (e.g. toilet roll tubes and yoghurt pots).

Learn to describe differences and similarities between different types of art.

Practise and develop techniques such as mixing colours, making patterns using geometric shapes, collaging with different textured materials and printing with vegetables.

Draw and paint to express their ideas and develop their imagination.

Learn about the work of a famous artist or designer — e.g. Wassily Kandinsky, Joan Miró or Henri Matisse.

The artwork your child does in class is often linked to a topic they're learning in that term — e.g. 'Seasons' or 'The Great Fire of London'.

Years 3 to 6

Your child will continue to improve their skill with different art, materials and techniques. They'll continue to experiment and express themselves creatively.

Your child might:

Get more practice with techniques such as drawing, painting and sculpture using different materials, e.g. charcoal, watercolours and wire.

Create a sketch book or art journal. These can be used to practise different techniques and make notes about pieces of art.

Learn about more great artists and designers such as Alberto Giacometti, L. S. Lowry and Henry Moore.

Although it might look like unpaid labour, getting Ayla involved with the decorating was simply about improving her painting skills...

How to help your child with Art and Design

Set up an art station at home where your child can practise their drawing, painting and sculpting (e.g. with Play-Doh®, plasticine or clay). This could be a specific area or just a box of art supplies and a protective sheet that can be used wherever.

Visit an art gallery and talk about what you see.

Create a gallery in your home (e.g. on the fridge) to celebrate your child's artwork.

Geography

In Geography children learn about different places in the world, how people live in these places and all about different environmental features. It's a big world out there so there's tonnes of interesting stuff to learn.

Reception, Year 1 & Year 2

Your child will learn about where they live, the rest of the UK and the world. This will include:

Places

- The <u>seven continents</u> and <u>five oceans</u> of the world.
- The <u>countries</u> of the UK, their <u>capital cities</u> and <u>surrounding areas</u>.
- The <u>differences</u> between a place in the UK and a <u>contrasting place</u> somewhere else in the world.

Features

- <u>Settlements</u> like cities, towns and villages.
- <u>Human</u> features such as <u>factories</u>, <u>farms</u> and <u>ports</u>.
- <u>Physical</u> features such as <u>beaches</u>, <u>hills</u> and <u>rivers</u>.
- <u>Seasons</u> and <u>weather patterns</u> in the UK.
- The <u>hot</u> and <u>cold</u> areas of the <u>world</u> (e.g. North & South Poles and deserts).

Key Concepts

- Getting to grips with various words used in Geography like <u>landmark</u>, <u>compass</u> and <u>country</u>.
- Using <u>observational skills</u> to study their surroundings.
- Using different <u>sources</u> of geographical information.

Geographical Skills

To build up their skills, they'll:

- use <u>maps</u>, <u>atlases</u> and <u>globes</u>.
- use <u>compass directions</u> (north, south, east and west) and other directional words such as near and far.
- use <u>aerial photos and plans</u> to recognise landmarks and features.
- learn to <u>draw simple maps</u> and create keys (symbols that represent real things on a map).
- carry out <u>simple fieldwork</u> to study features of their school and the local area, using equipment such as <u>rain gauges</u> and <u>thermometers</u>.

<u>Fieldwork</u> is learning directly in the real world outside the classroom.

Geography

Years 3 to 6

Your child will extend their knowledge and understanding of the UK and also learn about Europe, North America and South America, along with other significant geographical features of the world.

Places

- The locations of <u>different countries</u> in the world on maps and facts about them.

- The names and locations of UK <u>counties</u> and <u>cities</u>.

- The <u>physical features</u> and <u>land use</u> in different regions. E.g. mountains and sheep farming in the Lake District, and how land use has changed over time.

- The <u>similarities and differences</u> between a place in the UK and other places around the world.

- Lines of <u>latitude</u> and <u>longitude</u>, time zones and different regions of the world (such as the Arctic and Antarctic Circles).

This book* is great for learning facts about the UK. Not as tasty as grass though...

*part of CGP's Discover & Learn range

Features

- <u>Physical</u> aspects of geography including: <u>volcanoes</u>, <u>earthquakes</u>, <u>rivers</u>, <u>mountains</u> and the <u>water cycle</u>.

- <u>Human</u> aspects of geography such as: types of <u>settlement</u>, <u>land use</u> and how the <u>economy</u> works. Also how <u>natural resources</u>, such as <u>food</u>, <u>water</u> and <u>minerals</u> are <u>distributed</u>

Geographical Skills

- Learn more about <u>maps</u>, <u>atlases</u> and <u>globes</u> to build on knowledge from Years 1 and 2.

- Use the eight points of the <u>compass</u>.

- Interpret <u>Ordnance Survey maps</u> using grid references and scale.

- Carry out <u>more complex fieldwork</u> to collect, analyse and study geographical data such as <u>wind speed</u> and <u>light level</u>.

Key Concepts

- Getting to grips with words used in Geography like <u>biome</u>, <u>climate</u> and <u>vegetation belt</u>.

- Carry out more complex fieldwork to <u>observe</u>, <u>measure</u> and <u>record</u> the features of area.

- Use various <u>sources</u> of geographical information more <u>independently</u>.

A <u>biome</u> is a large area that contains a characteristic selection of plants and animals. The different types include forests (e.g. tropical rain forests) and aquatic (e.g. coral reefs).

Jen knew playing with superglue was a bad idea.

Geography

Learning Geography at school

At school your child might:

Visit local places such as woods, a castle or the coast.

Read stories in the news to learn more about climate change and what they can do to reduce their impact.

Go on residential trips.

Study local rivers.

Use geographical sources such as maps, photographs and the Google Earth™ mapping service, to discover more about their local environment.

Track major events around the world such as volcanoes, earthquakes and hurricanes.

Map the journey of the food they eat to find out where its ingredients have travelled from.

Write to a penpal in a contrasting area of the UK (e.g. in the countryside if your child goes to school in a city) or a different country.

"I took our daughter to see an exhibition on coastal erosion. For years after she was frightened our home would be destroyed by the sea. We lived in Birmingham at the time..."
— Cliff

CONFESSION CORNER

How to help your child with Geography

When you see news clips or videos about life in different countries, chat about what it might be like to live there compared to life in the UK.

Visit a landscape feature that your child has learnt about in class (e.g. a wood or a beach).

Have a map of the UK at home. Use it to talk about trips you've taken in the UK, the characteristics of different areas and test them on the names of counties and capital cities.

Talk about the changing seasons as they happen. Ask your child about how the weather differs between the seasons.

Plan a walk in your local area using a map. Talk through what the lines and symbols represent — if you don't know the answer use the key to find out together.

When travelling in the car or on the train, point out the rivers, cities and counties you pass through and visit.

Complete a jigsaw of a world map. Talk about where the different countries are in relation to each other (e.g. use compass directions and the names of continents). Can your child give a fact about any of them?

Mountains aren't just funny, they're hill areas...

Geography is all around us. Whenever you go out with your child keep an eye out for things that you can talk about. E.g. if you walk along a canal, you could describe that in the past they were used to transport goods.

Computing

Computing at school is about more than just using programs. Writing computer code (coding) and spotting mistakes in the code (debugging) are now expected — a bit different to word processing and playing solitaire.

Reception, Year 1 & Year 2

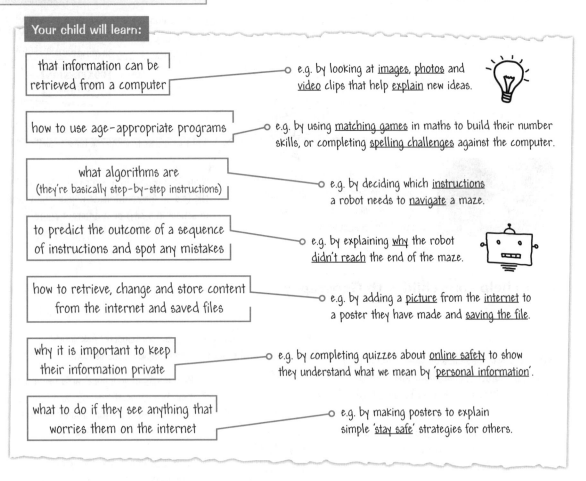

Your child will learn:

that information can be retrieved from a computer	e.g. by looking at images, photos and video clips that help explain new ideas.
how to use age-appropriate programs	e.g. by using matching games in maths to build their number skills, or completing spelling challenges against the computer.
what algorithms are (they're basically step-by-step instructions)	e.g. by deciding which instructions a robot needs to navigate a maze.
to predict the outcome of a sequence of instructions and spot any mistakes	e.g. by explaining why the robot didn't reach the end of the maze.
how to retrieve, change and store content from the internet and saved files	e.g. by adding a picture from the internet to a poster they have made and saving the file.
why it is important to keep their information private	e.g. by completing quizzes about online safety to show they understand what we mean by 'personal information'.
what to do if they see anything that worries them on the internet	e.g. by making posters to explain simple 'stay safe' strategies for others.

How can I help my child?

Take photos with a phone and show how they can be altered with filters or photo apps.

Allow supervised access to games and apps that your child can use to learn.

Teach your child how to interact with technology. E.g. how to use a mouse and to navigate through an eBook.

Teach your child what the different keys on a keyboard do. E.g. holding Shift and pressing a letter will type the capital.

Sometimes the Shift key is labelled with an arrow ⇧.

Computing

Years 3 to 6

Your child will learn:

to write simple programs to achieve a goal

e.g. making <u>simple games</u> where an on-screen character <u>moves</u>, interacts with its <u>surroundings</u> and responds to <u>commands</u>.

Unlike the characters on-screen Josh didn't respond to commands.

to spot errors in an algorithm and change them

e.g. when using coding apps like <u>Scratch</u>, children will be encouraged to find <u>mistakes</u> in their own algorithms.

to understand the variety of information and services available on the internet

e.g. they may learn how <u>online maps</u> work in Geography and about the benefits and dangers of <u>social media</u> in PSHE (p.79). This shows how computers play a part in <u>everyday life</u>.

to search for information effectively

e.g. using <u>inverted commas</u> in online searches (e.g. "Viking longboats") to search for a specific phrase and to use <u>keyboard shortcuts</u> like Ctrl + F to find a key word in a long piece of text.

to gather data and images and present them in new formats

e.g. research topics <u>independently</u> and present information in text, graphs and slideshows. They may even present their work by <u>writing for</u> the <u>school website</u> or by creating a <u>blog</u>.

to use technology safely and responsibly, and understand how concerns can be reported

e.g. <u>discussion</u>, <u>games</u> and <u>role-play</u> will all help children to know how to respond to <u>cyberbullying</u> or other possible threats to their <u>wellbeing</u> and <u>safety</u>.

How can I help my child?

Develop their creativity using apps like <u>Kids Doodle</u> for drawing or <u>Isle of Tune</u> for music making.

Talk to your child about how they would respond if faced with <u>images</u> they don't feel comfortable about on the internet. Take a look at the information on the <u>ThinkUKnow</u> website so that you can offer advice.

Give them opportunities to present their homework using apps like Microsoft® <u>Word</u> and Microsoft® <u>PowerPoint</u>®.

Build their typing speed with online tools like <u>Dance Mat Typing</u> which is free from BBC Bitesize.

Encourage them to try a free coding app like <u>Scratch</u>, <u>Code Club</u> or <u>Code Kingdoms</u> at home.

Just wait, in a few years your kids will be your tech support...

Nothing beats talking face-to-face with your child, however, apps and the internet can play a big part in how they learn. Look for apps and websites (e.g. MentalUP) that go beyond fun and require your child to solve challenges.

History

In History, your child will learn about the past and how it has affected our lives today. History lessons should make your child more curious about the past.

Steve suspected castles used to be a bit larger.

Reception, Year 1 & Year 2

Your child will learn about people and events, how they fit on to a timeline and their similarities and differences. They'll learn about:

Events before they were born

E.g.

- the Great Fire of London
- the first man on the moon
- the gunpowder plot
- the first aeroplane flight
- the sinking of the Titanic

Their own past

- What were they like as a baby?
- Has their family changed?
- Have they moved house?
- What toys did their grandparents used to play with? How are these different to their own toys nowadays?

Important people

E.g.

- Florence Nightingale, whose work as a nurse inspired many.
- Ernest Shackleton, who led three expeditions to the Antarctic.
- Rosa Parks, who fought for the rights of black people.

Where they live

- What historical events have happened here?
- Did any important people live or visit here?
- Are there places which tell us about the past here?

Linking historical events to places they know can make the past more relevant to your child.

Key Concepts

Your child will learn to:

- use words such as memories, decade, artefact, century, invention, explorer, evidence, generation and historical.

- understand ways that we find out about the past.

- use stories and other sources to show understanding.

A source is a historical item or document which tells us about the past. For example, a pot from Ancient Greece or a political cartoon from World War I.

History

Years 3 to 6

In Years 3 to 6 your child will learn more about local, national (British) and world history.

Early British history

- from the Stone Age to the Iron Age
- during the Roman Empire
- when the Anglo-Saxons and Scots settled
- from the Vikings to the Battle of Hastings

Recent British history

This might include:

- the Victorians
- changes in crime and punishment
- evacuation in World War II
- inventions of the last 150 years

Other Civilisations and Societies

This might include:

- Mayan civilisation
- Ancient Greece
- Ancient Egypt
- Early Islamic civilisation
- The Kingdom of Benin
- Indus Valley
- Shang Dynasty

For more about British History and Civilisations, look for CGP's Discover & Learn range.

Your child will study their local area in more detail and discover how national history is reflected in where they live — e.g. they might research how many young men in the local area went to fight in World War I and how many of them returned.

Key Concepts

Your child will learn to:

- use terms such as empire, archaeologist, invasion and chronological order.
- understand connections, contrasts and trends over time.
- determine whether sources of evidence are reliable or biased.

History

Learning History at school

At school your child may:

take part in a dress-up day

use drama to act out events in history — e.g. pretending to be in a Victorian school room, following the rules of the time

use historical sources such as newspapers, artefacts (in class or in museums), diaries and photographs

visit a place of historical interest

take part in history workshops — e.g. building a model pyramid and learning about how they were constructed

interview or write to an important person or a historian

analyse and evaluate historical sources for reliability

How to help your child with History

Take a walk locally and look at the different types of buildings. Try and work out how old they are by looking for clues about when they were built.

Make a family tree. Ask relatives questions to help with names, dates and places.

Take a trip to a national museum to find out about the history of a wide range of people and places. Museums like the British Museum offer online tours so you can learn from home.

Take a trip to a local museum to find out more about the history of your local area.

Go to your local library and borrow some books about ancient civilizations like the Greeks, the Egyptians or the Mayans.

Create a photo album of your child and talk to them about how their life has changed so much already.

Watch history programmes, such as Horrible Histories, and children's films based in historical settings, e.g. Hercules or Mary Poppins. Talk with your child about similarities and differences with their own life and what they watched.

The Dark Age had a lot of long knights...

You don't have to travel far in the UK to find something of historical significance. Even if you don't have a Roman fortress or Norman castle on your doorstep, it's likely there'll be some ancient structures (e.g. churches) nearby.

Religious Education

Although Religious Education (RE) isn't on the National Curriculum, it's compulsory for it to be taught in state schools. Most schools follow a locally agreed curriculum which you can ask to see a copy of.

Which faiths might my child learn about?

While the teaching should reflect that Britain is traditionally a Christian country, it should also give an insight into the beliefs and practices of a variety of faiths.

> The RE taught in your child's school may vary depending on whether it's a faith school (see page 3) or not. A faith school may occasionally take part in special services or have assemblies with a more religious theme.

Faith	Christianity	Islam	Judaism	Hinduism	Sikhism	Humanism
Followers	Christians	Muslims	Jews	Hindus	Sikhs	Humanists
Holy Book	Bible	Qur'an	Torah	The Vedas	Guru Granth Sahib	No specific text
Place of Worship	Church	Mosque	Synagogue	Temple	Gurdwara	No specific place

> Your child might not learn about all of the faiths shown above — this will depend on the faiths your child's school have chosen to teach about. The aim of teaching about different faiths is to promote understanding and tolerance rather than promoting any particular belief.

What might my child do in RE?

Visit a synagogue (a Jewish place of worship) or other place of worship to learn about the unique features of the building.

Draw the symmetrical patterns used to decorate mosque (a Muslim place of worship).

Learn which symbols are associated with different faiths.

Make foods associated with religious festivals like barfi for Diwali (the Hindu Festival of Light).

Take part in the school Nativity play — which is all about the birth of Jesus.

Compare festivals for birth, marriage or death across different faiths.

> Parents have the right to withdraw their child from some or all RE activities, including special celebrations (like Christian hymns or Eid). It's a good idea to talk to the school about what they plan to teach if you have any concerns.

God said 'Come forth', but John came 5ᵗʰ and won a toaster...

Religion can be a sensitive subject. Teaching your child to be curious but not rude is important. Explain to your child that it's OK to ask people about their faith to learn more about it but they should do so in a respectful way.

Foreign Languages

Foreign Languages is a compulsory subject at Key Stage 2 (Years 3 to 6). Each school is free to choose which language they would like to teach. Although French and Spanish are the usual favourites, your child's school might teach something a bit more unusual like Mandarin Chinese or Japanese.

What your child might learn each year

Year 3
- Understand and learn a <u>few familiar words</u> and <u>short phrases</u>.
- Have a go at spelling <u>key words</u>.
- Repeat a phrase <u>changing</u> a single word.

> J'ai <u>sept</u> ans.
> *I am <u>7</u> years old.*

> J'ai <u>huit</u> ans.
> *I am <u>8</u> years old.*

Year 4
- <u>Pick out words</u> they understand from a conversation.
- Use <u>common phrases</u> in role play.
- Read and write <u>simple phrases</u>.

> Comment t'appelles-tu?
> *What is your name?*

> Je m'appelle Sean.
> *My name is Sean.*

Year 5
- Understand the <u>main points</u> from a short passage of speech.
- <u>Ask</u> and <u>answer questions</u> on a topic.
- Follow the <u>grammar rules</u> of their new language.

English	the
French	le / la / les

	Past	Present
English	I was hungry	I am hungry
French	J'avais faim	J'ai faim

Découvrez la série 'Practise & Learn' pour les langues, de CGP. Check out CGP's Languages Practise & Learn series.

Year 6
- Speak in <u>longer sentences</u> and <u>create some of their own</u> to ask questions or describe a picture.
- Write a short text in <u>simple sentences</u>.
- Read short passages <u>aloud</u> to improve their <u>pronunciation</u>.
- Use a <u>dictionary</u> or <u>translation tool</u> to find new words.

> Voici mon chien Harry. Harry est brun avec des oreilles blanches. Il aime jouer dans le parc.
>
> *This is my dog Harry. Harry is brown with white ears. He likes to play in the park.*

How can I help my child?

<u>Vocabulary posters</u> in the bedroom can be great for <u>building</u> a bank of useful words.

There are lots of fantastic <u>apps</u> to <u>help</u> children learn a new language. <u>Penyo Pal</u>, <u>Duolingo Kids</u> and <u>Gus on the Go</u> are just some of those suitable for phones or tablets.

Stick Post-It® Notes on objects <u>around the house</u> with the language word on them — e.g. on their bedroom door, 'ma chambre'.

Music

In Music, your child will learn how music is created and listen to a variety of types of music. They'll get the opportunity to sing, dance, compose music and learn how to play instruments. Who knows, it could turn into a great hobby or even a career — who doesn't want to see their name in lights?

Reception, Year 1 & Year 2

Your child will develop their skills in Music by moving to music, using their voice, listening to music and making sounds using instruments. They'll be taught:

Moving

to freestyle, learn routines and hear the beat of the music.

Singing

* to sing songs.
* to express emotion through their singing.
* to speak in chants and rhymes.

Playing

* to play tuned instruments such as recorders, xylophones and chime bars.
* to play untuned percussion instruments such as tambourines, drums and triangles.
* to experiment with and combine sounds — e.g. using different pitch, rhythm and sound.

Listening

to listen to a range of music and be able to talk about what they hear — e.g. different voices and instruments.

It's a great idea for children to listen to both recorded and live music. Your child may get the chance to see musicians perform live at school.

The school drum teacher really hoped George could hold onto the sticks this time.

How can I help my child?

Encourage your child to move to the music they hear — a good way of doing this is by demonstrating... Try and hide any inhibitions and wiggle to the beat to show how it's done.

Play music when you're at home or in the car and talk about the instruments, voices and style of the music. Ask them what they like listening to and why. Perhaps you could play some of your favourite songs and talk about them.

Create homemade instruments using household objects or materials from the recycling.

Chat about the sounds you hear when you're out and about like birdsong, car engine noise and the sound of wind moving through trees. Discuss how loud or quiet, and how high or low pitched they are.

Music

Years 3 to 6

Your child will learn to play instruments and sing more confidently. They'll be able to create music and you're likely to get to see them perform on the school stage at some point. They'll be taught:

Singing

- to sing <u>solo</u> and with <u>others</u>.
- to perform with <u>confidence</u>.

Playing

- to play instruments with a <u>greater level of skill</u>.
- to continue <u>experimenting with</u> and <u>combining sounds</u>.

Listening

- to listen to music and be able to <u>respond</u> to what they hear — e.g. recognising specific <u>instruments</u> recalling different <u>rhythms</u>.
- to appreciate a wide range of <u>live</u> and <u>recorded</u> music from different traditions, composers and musicians.
- to develop an understanding of the <u>history</u> of music.

Composing

- to <u>improvise</u> and <u>compose</u> music for a range of purposes — e.g. to present a weather forecast or to represent the journey of a river.
- to use and understand <u>written music</u>.

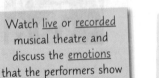

If your child is interested in learning an instrument, speak to the school's head of music. They can arrange for a specialist music teacher to come into school to teach your child on a one to one basis. Music lessons are unlikely to be free, but the school may be able to contribute towards the cost.

How can I help my child?

Watch <u>live</u> or <u>recorded</u> musical theatre and discuss the <u>emotions</u> that the performers show through their singing.

Listen to a <u>wide range</u> of music and talk about how music has <u>changed</u> since you were younger.

Sing songs <u>together</u> at home and on journeys. You could even <u>add actions</u> for fun.

Introduce them to music-making apps such as <u>GarageBand</u> and <u>MusiQuest</u>.

Show them pictures of equipment for playing music such as a <u>gramophone</u>, <u>record player</u>, <u>cassette player</u>, <u>CD player</u> and an <u>MP3 player</u>. Talk to them about the differences and perhaps which ones you've used in the past.

See live music <u>locally</u> — this is a great way to teach your child how to be a <u>respectful audience member</u>.

Sweet dreams are made of cheese, who am I to diss a Brie?

Listening to different types of music with your child is great for increasing their knowledge of music. It might be useful in other ways too — e.g. listening to classical music can help relax your child before bedtime. Win win.

Physical Education

Your child will do some sort of Physical Education (PE) at least twice a week at primary school. Whether they look forward to it or are glad when it's over, it's a legal requirement so there's no getting out of it...

Reception, Year 1 & Year 2

Your child will:

- use equipment such as bats, skipping ropes and hula hoops to improve their agility and coordination.

- learn to roll, aim, throw and catch — this might be done using a balloon, a beanbag or a tennis ball, etc.

- take part in team games such as cricket or football. They'll learn simple ways of attacking and defending and also get experience of winning and losing graciously.

- learn to move in different ways and directions in the space around them — e.g. by moving like particular animals or by playing 'Cat and Mouse' or 'What's the time Mr Wolf?'.

- develop control of their body when balancing. For example, they might practise balancing on their bottom, on their tummy or on one leg. They'll use gymnastics equipment such as benches to balance on.

- learn, practise and perform sequences of movements to music. These dances could re-tell well known stories like the Hare and the Tortoise or they may link to what they're learning in Science (e.g. springs and magnets) or in RE (e.g. the festival of Diwali).

Make sure all PE kit (and uniform) has your child's name in it. Some clothes have space on the label for writing a name in pen, or you can get printed name tags to sew or iron on. Use a black marker for writing their names inside pumps and school shoes.

How to help your child with PE

Enjoy family walks together. These can be made more engaging by 'treasure hunting' for a list of things.

Have fun with your child in water — even being able to put their face in the water will help them when they learn to swim at a later date.

Get involved in local parkruns with your child (or just make up your own running routes).

At the weekends and during school holidays, make sure your child gets some exercise outside every day.

Help your child to learn to ride a bike.

Encourage your child to join after-school sports or local sports clubs if a particular sport interests them.

Government guidelines say that children should be physically active for an average of at least 60 minutes per day across the week.

Physical Education

Years 3 to 6

Your child will continue to develop their control, balance, flexibility and agility. They'll also reflect on what they do well and how they could improve. Your child will:

- warm up before exercising (and understand why it's important to do so).

- take part in activities that involve running, jumping, catching or throwing (or combinations of them). They'll also take part in athletic activities such as running, long jump and javelin throwing.

- know the skills needed to attack and defend in a variety of games.

- learn the rules for games such as badminton, netball, cricket, basketball, hockey, football, rounders, tennis, etc.

- develop their skills in gymnastics and dance.

- create and refine gymnastic or dance sequences using the floor, freestanding equipment (e.g. benches) and fixed equipment (e.g. wall bars).

- be encouraged to reach their personal best, such as their time to run 100 m.

Your child's school may take part in 'The Daily Mile' — an international project that gets all children moving to improve both physical and mental health.

Zoe believed she could fly... Luckily, there was a crash mat below.

Swimming lessons

- By the time your child leaves primary school, they should have taken part in some swimming lessons.

- Not many schools have their own swimming pool so they're usually held in a local swimming pool.

- As lessons are given by specialist swimming teachers, you may have to pay something towards it.

- Your child should leave primary school able to:

  - ☑ swim for at least 25 metres confidently.

  - ☑ swim breaststroke, backstroke and front crawl.

  - ☑ understand the importance of safety in water and know how to float on their back.

This is like the 'cycling proficiency' which you might've done at school.

Bikeability

- Year 6 children are often given the opportunity to take part in a cycling training programme.

- It'll probably be held at school, usually in school time.

- Again, as it's usually run by specialists, you'll probably have to pay a bit towards it.

The school will have a policy on earrings in PE — e.g. they may have to be covered with a plaster or the child must be able to remove them.

Speak to your child's school if you are concerned about being able to afford either of these activities — they're often able to offer support if needed.

I hope you're hapPE with this information...

It's easier for girls when getting dressed after PE if they don't have the hassle of putting tights back on. So on days they have PE it's a good idea to send them to school in socks instead.

PSHE

Personal, Social, Health and Economic Education (PSHE) is split into three main areas at primary school.

Health and wellbeing

Your child might learn:

What makes us feel good

- E.g. by discussing the benefits of playing outside and getting enough sleep. zzZ

- Older children could present their ideas of how they can deal with strong emotions like anxiety.

How to stay healthy and safe

- E.g. about the value of healthy eating and exercise.

- Older children will learn about the dangers of drugs, alcohol and smoking.

How we change as we grow older

- E.g. about how our needs and responsibilities change with age.

- Older children will discuss the physical and emotional changes of puberty as well as the importance of good personal hygiene.

Relationships

Your child might learn:

For more on what the school might cover in Relationships and Sex Education, take a look at pages 27-28.

What's a safe relationship

- E.g. that talking to a trusted adult about anything that makes them feel uncomfortable is the right thing to do.

- Older children will complete activities to remind them of the dos and don'ts of talking with others online.

What's important in a family

- E.g. by writing about the support they receive from different family members.

- Older children will learn that caring relationships aren't limited to traditional 'mum and dad' families.

What makes a good friendship

- E.g. by sharing simple strategies to fix disagreements or make new friends.

- Older children will talk about peer pressure and recognise what a healthy friendship looks like.

Living in the wider world

Your child might learn:

What jobs adults do

- E.g. by meeting visitors to school and role-playing different jobs.

- Older children will research the skills and qualifications needed for jobs they would like to do.

The role of money in our lives

- E.g. by playing shop and identifying the difference between 'wants' and 'needs'.

- Older children will consider spending decisions that can affect others — like giving to charity or buying Fairtrade.

How we can look after the natural world

- E.g. about the importance of creating wildlife friendly areas.

- Older children will learn about shared responsibilities like recycling and preventing pollution.

Why did the student eat his homework? It was a piece of cake...

Taking a positive approach to living a healthy and safe life rather than shocking or guilting your child into behaving a certain way will help in the long run. Having a positive outlook on food and money, etc. will help in their future.

Assessment Overview

Your child will have a handful of assessments whilst they're at primary school and this section of the book is here to give you the lowdown. Before we get into it, here's a map of what they'll be going through...

RECEPTION BASELINE ASSESSMENT ✖
This assessment gives a snapshot of your child's skills when they first start school — see page 81.

INFANTS ISLAND

PHONICS ✖ **SCREENING CHECK**
This test assesses your child's phonics skills. It happens in Year 1 — see page 82

KS1 SATS ✖
Tests taken at the end of Year 2 to assess your child's progress in Maths and English — see pages 83-84.

KS2 SATS ✖
Tests taken at the end of Year 6 to assess your child's progress in core subjects before secondary school — see pages 86-87.

ISLE OF JUNIORS

✖ **TIMES TABLE CHECK**
This test assesses your child's knowledge of their times tables. It happens in Year 4 — see page 85.

✖ **11+**
These optional tests must be passed to get into certain secondary schools — see pages 88-89. They're taken in Year 6.

What happens if you take the p out of a pirate? They become irate...

That reminds me — a pirate outfit is pretty easy to rustle up if you're struggling for a fancy dress day. Put a large white shirt on them tied with a black belt and pop a bandanna on. Sorted. For more fancy dress ideas see p.20.

Reception Baseline Assessment

The Reception Baseline Assessment (RBA) assesses a child's early abilities when they first start primary school. Read on to find out about what it is and what it's for.

What is the Reception Baseline Assessment?

1) The RBA is a <u>short assessment</u> that children take in Reception.

2) It's done in the <u>first 6 weeks</u> of Reception, takes around <u>20 minutes</u> and is done one-on-one with their teacher or a teaching assistant.

3) This will be done in <u>class</u> and your child probably <u>won't know</u> they're taking an assessment.

4) The RBA provides a <u>snapshot</u> of your child's skills in:

- <u>Maths</u>
- <u>Communication</u>
- <u>Language</u>
- <u>Literacy</u>

5) There are <u>a range of different question types</u> that your child might answer by:

- giving a <u>verbal</u> response.
- <u>pointing</u> out the correct answer.
- <u>ordering</u> or <u>moving</u> objects around.

6) The assessment can be <u>altered</u> to suit a child's ability. For example, if a child is struggling the teacher could switch to asking a <u>simpler set</u> of questions.

"The school rang me when my son was in Reception to let me know he'd tried to eat his shoe... I think they were worried he wasn't getting all his nutrients..." — Lacey

CONFESSION CORNER

This learning malarkey is tiring...

Children with SEND (p.29-30) or those with EAL (p.26) will still be able to take the RBA but the teacher will adapt the test for them.

What is it for?

1) The RBA is used to measure the <u>performance of the school</u>. The scores of the children in your child's class will be <u>compared</u> against how well they do <u>later on in primary school</u> — particularly in the KS2 SATs (see p.86). This will give an indication of <u>how well children are progressing</u> at your child's school.

2) The reception teacher will also receive an <u>assessment summary</u> for each child. This shows whether or not they need to give any <u>extra help</u> to your child in their first term. The assessment summary is a set of <u>short</u>, <u>written statements</u> of how well your child did.

Why did the kid cross the playground? To get to the other slide...

They start them young on assessments these days. There's no need to worry about the RBA though, as it's just to measure what level your child is at when they start school. It's not time to get out the revision guides just yet...

Phonics Screening Check

For a reminder of what Phonics is, take a look back at pages 31 and 32 before heading into this page about how it's assessed. The Phonics Screening Check tests your child's phonics skills at primary.

What is the Phonics Screening Check?

1) The Phonics Screening Check is a <u>short test</u> that children take towards the end of Year 1. It's done <u>one-to-one</u> with the <u>teacher</u>.

2) The Check is designed to ensure each child has <u>mastered</u> the <u>phonics skills</u> expected for their age, and can be used to help identify areas where they may need <u>additional support</u>.

What is covered in the Check?

1) The Check contains 40 words which the child is asked to <u>read aloud</u>. It is divided into <u>two sections</u>, each containing 20 words. The second section is more challenging than the first.

2) Within each section are <u>real words</u> and <u>pseudo-words</u> (words that aren't real). Some of the real words are less common than others, so may be new to the child.

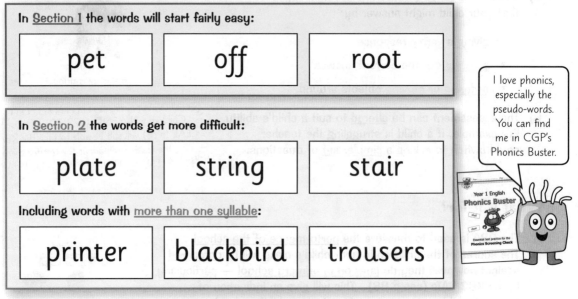

In <u>Section 1</u> the words will start fairly easy:

pet   off   root

In <u>Section 2</u> the words get more difficult:

plate   string   stair

Including words with <u>more than one syllable</u>:

printer   blackbird   trousers

> I love phonics, especially the pseudo-words. You can find me in CGP's Phonics Buster.

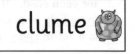

3) The pseudo-words are <u>new to all children</u> and allow them to demonstrate their phonics skills <u>independently</u> of any <u>visual memory</u> of words or <u>vocabulary knowledge</u>.

4) Next to each pseudo-word is a picture of an <u>imaginary creature</u>. During the Check, the child will be told that the word is the name of the imaginary creature.

clume

Rejected word for the Phonics Check #6982: Antidisestablishmentarianism...

Reading with your child is a great way to put their phonics skills to the test. The more reading they do, the faster they'll get to grips with segmenting and blending as described on page 31.

KS1 SATs

SATs are national tests set by the government that are used to measure a child's progress in primary school. They're taken in May at the end of Year 2 (KS1 SATs) and Year 6 (KS2 SATs).

See p.86-87 for information about the KS2 SATs.

KS1 SATs test English and Maths

1) Although SATs have to be taken in May, schools can set their own timetable. They're often worked into normal classroom activities and some children might not even know they've sat them.

2) None of the tests are strictly timed — your child's teacher will make sure all pupils have an appropriate amount of time to complete each test.

3) Children do tests for Maths and English (which might include optional ones in Spelling, Punctuation and Grammar) but not for other subjects, e.g. Science. Instead, these other subjects are assessed by your child's teacher throughout the school year without a formal test.

> The government has announced that KS1 SATs will become non-statutory from 2023. This means that schools will be able to choose whether to do them or not. The government does change its mind about assessments from time to time — you can find updates on gov.uk. Or just ask your child's teacher whether they'll be doing KS1 SATs.

English

Your child will complete two Reading papers:
- Both papers have a combination of fiction and non-fiction texts.
- The texts and questions get progressively harder for both papers.
- The teacher can ask your child to complete up to a certain question number in the test which corresponds with their ability level.

Reading paper 1
- takes about 30 minutes
- is worth 20 marks
- has a short piece of text and questions relating to that text on each page
- might have some useful words at the start.

The sample questions you see on these pages are taken from CGP's SATs practice paper range.

Reading paper 2
- takes about 40 minutes
- is worth 20 marks
- contains large pieces of text with questions relating to each text in a separate booklet.

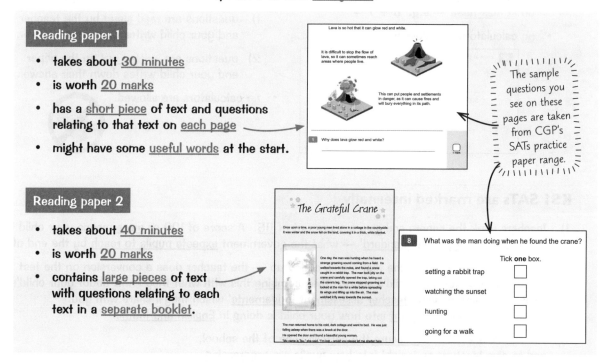

KS1 SATs

Spelling, Punctuation and Grammar (two optional papers)

There are some free SATs resources on the CGP website. Check them out using the link below* or this QR code.

Spelling

- takes about <u>15 minutes</u>
- there are <u>20 spellings to do</u>
- the teacher <u>reads out a word</u> and uses it in a sentence
- your child will have the <u>same sentence</u> in their answer booklet with a <u>gap</u> where the <u>word</u> they need to <u>spell</u> should go.

Grammar, Punctuation & Spelling

- takes about <u>20 minutes</u>
- is worth <u>20 marks</u>
- questions <u>could include</u> joining two words together to make one (e.g. 'white' and 'board' to make whiteboard) or choosing which sentence needs a question mark, etc.

Maths

Your child will complete <u>two</u> Maths papers:

Arithmetic

- takes about <u>20 minutes</u>
- is worth <u>25 marks</u>
- contains questions that your child will do <u>in their head</u> — e.g. '6 + 7 ='
- <u>no</u> calculators are allowed.

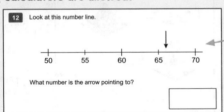

Reasoning

- takes about <u>35 minutes</u>
- is worth <u>35 marks</u>
- is split into <u>two sections</u>
  1) questions are <u>read aloud</u> by the teacher and your child writes down their answer.
  2) questions are <u>written out</u> on the paper and your child writes down their answer.
- <u>no</u> calculators are allowed.

KS1 SATs are marked internally

1) <u>Teachers</u> mark the papers and give a score out of <u>115</u>. A score of <u>100 or more</u> means your child is working at the '<u>expected standard</u>' — what the government <u>expects pupils to reach</u> by the end of KS1.

2) The score of 115 isn't just the test marks added up — the teacher does a conversion on the test results to <u>work out</u> your child's score. They <u>combine</u> this with what they know about your child's abilities to come up with '<u>teacher assessment judgements</u>' which they'll share with you. These will give you an <u>insight</u> into how your child is doing in <u>English and Maths</u>.

3) The scores are used to <u>measure the performance</u> of the school, and to give teachers an insight into <u>how pupils are progressing</u>.

*https://www.cgpbooks.co.uk/primarysatsresources

Times Table Check

The Times Table Check, or Multiplication Tables Check (MTC), is a short test to see how well your child can do their times tables. Just like back in the day, kids still need to learn their times tables.

What is the Times Table Check?

1) The Check is a test of <u>25 times table questions</u>.

2) It includes questions on the <u>2 times table</u> up to the <u>12 times table</u>.

3) It's the <u>first compulsory test</u> in England that'll be sat <u>using an electronic device</u> — e.g. a computer or tablet.

When is the Times Table Check?

The Check was introduced in 2021 but is only compulsory from 2022.

1) Children take the Check in <u>Year 4</u> and it'll take most of them <u>no longer</u> than <u>5 minutes</u> to complete.

2) Your child will have <u>6 seconds</u> to answer each question followed by a <u>3 second</u> break before the next one.

3) Each year, the Check will be taken in <u>June</u>.

4) Teachers have the option of delivering the Check to <u>individuals</u>, <u>groups</u> within the class or the <u>whole class</u> at the same time.

What is the Times Table Check for?

You can test your child on their times tables by using CGP's handy free Times Table Tester. Use the link below* or just scan this QR code.

Tables Tester

1) The Check is designed to make sure each child has <u>mastered</u> the times tables <u>expected for their age</u>, and can be used to show where they may need <u>additional support</u> with them.

2) Schools are obliged to let parents or guardians know <u>how their child has done</u> in the Check.

3) From 2022, schools will be able to use the results of the Check to <u>compare themselves</u> locally and nationally with other schools (and see if they could improve).

Monique could see why the abacus was a useful learning tool but couldn't imagine Leo would use it much after being introduced to a little thing called a calculator...

 ×  =

You don't need to do anything specific to prepare your child for the Times Table Check but it's always a great idea to practise the times tables with your child. Just a few minutes every day can help your child learn them.

*https://www.cgpbooks.co.uk/times-table-tester

Testing & Assessment

KS2 SATs

There's no doubt about it, Key Stage 2 SATs are a bigger deal than the Key Stage 1 SATs. But don't worry, we've compiled loads of useful information so you know what the KS2 SATs are all about.

KS2 SATs test Maths and English

1) The government <u>set a date</u> for the SATs to happen and the tests <u>must happen</u> on that date, usually in <u>May</u>.

2) Unlike at KS1, your child will sit the tests in <u>exam conditions</u> — your child's teacher will make sure they're <u>prepared</u> for this.

3) Children do tests for <u>Maths</u> and <u>English</u>, and potentially for <u>Science</u> too (described below and on the next page). <u>English writing</u> is <u>assessed separately</u> by teachers using the writing your child does throughout the year.

4) Completed papers are sent away to be <u>marked externally</u> and are given a score out of <u>120</u>. A score of 100 or more means your child is working at the '<u>expected standard</u>' — what the government <u>expects pupils to reach</u> by the end of KS2. A score of 110 or more means your child is considered to be '<u>working at greater depth</u>'.

5) The scores are also used to measure the <u>performance of the school</u>, <u>pupils' progress</u> and to help put pupils into <u>ability groups</u> when they start secondary school.

6) There are <u>no SATs</u> for any other subjects, such as Computing and Foreign Languages. These subjects are <u>assessed by your child's teacher</u> throughout the school year without a formal test.

Maths

Your child will sit <u>three</u> Maths papers:

Arithmetic

- takes <u>30 minutes</u>
- is worth <u>40 marks</u>
- has <u>different</u> types of sums, from <u>addition</u> and <u>subtraction</u> questions worth <u>1 mark</u> to <u>long division</u> and <u>long multiplication</u> worth <u>2 marks</u>.

Reasoning

There are <u>two</u> papers, each one:

- takes <u>40 minutes</u>
- is worth <u>35 marks</u>
- has <u>different types</u> of questions on <u>mathematical reasoning</u>, including <u>multiple choice</u>, <u>drawing a shape</u>, <u>true or false</u> and more.

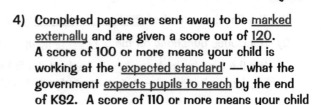

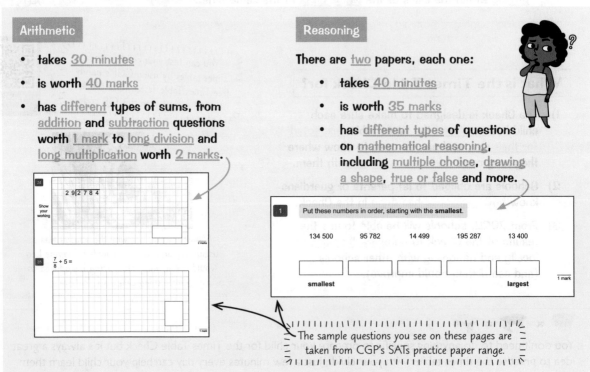

The sample questions you see on these pages are taken from CGP's SATs practice paper range.

KS2 SATs

English

Your child will sit <u>three</u> English papers:

Grammar, Punctuation and Spelling

- takes <u>45 minutes</u>
- is worth <u>50 marks</u>
- has a mixture of <u>multiple choice</u> questions and questions with <u>short answers</u>.

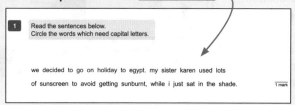

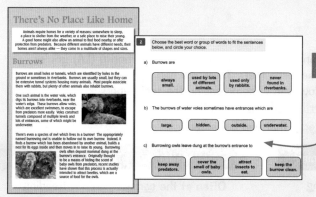

There are some free SATs resources on the CGP website. Check them out using the link below* or this QR code.

Spelling

- takes <u>15 minutes</u>
- there are <u>20 spellings</u> to do
- the teacher <u>reads out a word</u> and uses it in sentence
- your child will have the <u>same sentence</u> in their answer booklet with a <u>gap</u> where the <u>word</u> they need to <u>spell</u> should go.

Reading

- takes <u>1 hour</u>, including reading time
- is worth <u>50 marks</u>
- contains <u>three large pieces</u> of text with questions relating to each text in a <u>separate booklet</u>.

Science

Every two years around <u>2000 schools</u> are selected to do Science SATs — these tests are done to <u>sample</u> how well children are doing in Science <u>nationally</u>. If your child's school is selected, <u>fewer than 10 children</u> per school take the test, but if your child *is* chosen (lucky them), here's some more information:

- The test is split into <u>three</u> papers: <u>Biology</u>, <u>Chemistry</u> and <u>Physics</u>.
- Each paper takes <u>25 minutes</u>.
- Each paper is worth <u>22 marks</u>.
- Questions explore a child's <u>Science knowledge</u> — e.g. giving two things that plants need to grow.

The school doesn't receive these results. They're marked externally and the data is used to assess national Science standards.

Favourite pencil in hand, Abigail was ready to tackle whatever the SATs could throw at her.

*https://www.cgpbooks.co.uk/primarysatsresources

11+

It can be tricky to find reliable information about the 11+ and how to prepare for it.
These pages cover the basics — what the 11+ test is and how it works.

The 11+ is a selective test

Most secondary schools in the UK are <u>comprehensive</u>
— they accept children of <u>all abilities</u>. But in some
areas, <u>selective state secondary schools</u> (grammar
schools) still exist and the <u>11+ test</u> is used to
determine if a child is <u>suitable</u> for them. The 11+ test
is also used for entry to some independent schools.

Children usually sit the test in the <u>first term</u> of their
<u>last year at primary school</u>. Some schools select
pupils based just on the <u>11+ test results</u>, but others
look at <u>other factors</u>, e.g. whether you live close to
the school, or if you have other children at the school.

Check out our 11+
range to help your
child prepare for
any test on the 11+.

The format of the test varies

The exact <u>format</u> of the 11+ test <u>varies</u> depending on the school or Local Authority (LA) you're
applying to, as well as on the provider that sets the test. There are <u>two main test providers</u>
for the 11+ — <u>GL Assessment</u> and <u>CEM</u>. However, in some cases, the test papers
will be written by the <u>school</u>, or by a <u>consortium of schools</u> in that area.

Wherever you are, there are <u>four main subjects</u> that can be tested:

Non-Verbal Reasoning	Verbal Reasoning	Maths	English
<u>Problem-solving</u> using <u>pictures</u> and <u>symbols</u>.	<u>Problem-solving</u> and <u>logic</u> using <u>words</u>, <u>letters</u>, etc.	Often at the <u>same</u> <u>level</u> as the <u>SATs</u>, but it may be <u>more challenging</u>.	Reading <u>comprehension</u>, <u>grammar</u> and sometimes a <u>writing</u> task.

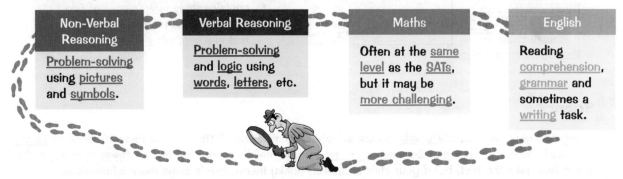

The tests are usually either <u>multiple choice</u> or <u>standard answer</u> format.

- <u>Multiple choice</u> — there may be a <u>separate answer sheet</u>. There's usually a choice of
four or five options for each answer, and the answers are often computer-marked.

- <u>Standard answer</u> — there are <u>spaces on the question paper</u> for the pupil to write their
<u>own answers</u>. There will <u>not</u> usually be any <u>answer options</u> given for the pupil to choose from.

Make sure you know <u>which provider</u> is responsible for the test in your area, and find out <u>as</u>
<u>much information</u> as you can about the <u>format</u> of the test <u>before you start</u> preparing for it.

11+

The 11+ is different in each area

- In some areas, <u>every child</u> who wants to go to grammar school sits the <u>same test</u> which is organised by the LA. Your child might be entered for this test <u>automatically</u>. In other areas, you'll need to apply to each grammar school <u>individually</u>, and your child will sit a <u>separate test</u> for <u>each school</u> you've applied to.

- Even in areas where the LA handles entry for the majority of grammar schools, there may still be some schools which <u>must be</u> applied for <u>separately</u>. These schools may also set a separate test.

Admission rules can be complicated

- The <u>rules</u> that schools use to <u>allocate their places</u> are <u>complicated</u>, and they can affect your child's chance of getting a place. <u>Every school</u> you apply to will have its own <u>admissions policy</u>. Familiarise yourself with each one so you know how <u>realistic</u> your <u>child's chances</u> of being <u>offered a place</u> are.

- Some selective schools allocate places based on '<u>best mark first</u>'. Children are <u>ranked</u> in order of their test marks, and <u>places are offered</u> to the children at the <u>top of the list</u>. However, many set an 11+ '<u>pass mark</u>' then <u>allocate places</u> to children who <u>score higher than this mark</u> based on <u>other criteria</u> such as distance from the school and whether they have a sibling already in the school.

- Many grammar schools are <u>oversubscribed</u>, which means that your child <u>might not be offered a place</u> even if they <u>reach the 11+ pass mark</u>. For example, if the school prioritises children who live close to the school but you live some distance away.

Research each school you apply to

Here's a list of things you'll need to know about the schools you apply to:

1. <u>How to enter for the test</u> — whether you have to send off any <u>paperwork</u> to enter your child into the test (and when the deadline for this is), or whether they'll be entered <u>automatically</u>.

2. <u>What's in the test</u> — what <u>subjects</u> will be <u>tested</u> (Verbal Reasoning, Maths, etc.).

3. <u>What's the test format</u> — the <u>format</u> the test will take (<u>multiple choice</u> or <u>standard answer</u>) and <u>how long</u> the test will last.

4. <u>Where</u> and <u>when</u> the test will be.

5. <u>Any other admissions criteria</u> — e.g. <u>distance</u> from the school, <u>siblings</u> at the school, etc.

6. <u>Whether past papers or mock tests are available</u> — some schools publish <u>past test papers</u> or organise <u>mock tests</u>. They'll often charge a fee though.

Check out the CGP website using the link below* or scan this QR code — there are loads of free resources for the 11+.

11+

I always thought 11+ just meant anyone older than 11...

Exams can be stressful at any age, and add trying to get into a specific school into the mix and your 11-year-old might feel the pressure. Alleviate some of that by making sure they still get fresh air and see their friends.

Choosing a Secondary School

If you have a selection of secondary schools to choose from in your area, you'll need to decide which you'd prefer for your child. The process is similar to the one you went through to apply for a primary school place.

Start getting prepared early

The application deadline is 31st October
Your child's school should share information from the local education authority with you in September, shortly after your child starts in Year 6 — it's then over to you to complete the application form.

If you live in a grammar school area
You need to decide if you want your child to sit the 11+ test — they need to be registered for it when they're still in Year 5 (as early as May in some areas). You'll also have to fill in a form listing selective and non-selective schools by 31st October.

In some areas you have to fill in the 11+ registration form yourself, but in others, all children are automatically registered (but you can opt them out).

Do your research

1) Visiting the schools is a must. There'll probably be a headteacher's speech, but talking to the students who are helping out will give you an honest view of the school.

2) Talk with your child about their preferences.

3) Look at the website of each school to find out what they offer, e.g. the languages taught and the sports facilities available.

4) Check the admissions criteria for the schools you are interested in. They'll be based on factors such as how far you live from the school, and whether your child has a sibling already attending the school.

5) Consider how your child will get to each school. Is public transport available? How much will it cost?

There is no way I'm wearing that uniform!

You don't have to limit yourself to the schools in your local authority area, particularly if you live close to the border.

You might be eligible for free transport — check with your local authority.

Golden rules for applying for a secondary school place

1) Read everything carefully and supply all the documents asked for.

You might need to include a utility bill to prove your address — check if it has to be the original or if a photo will do.

Faith schools often ask for extras that you're expected to send to them, e.g. a baptism certificate or evidence of church attendance.

Only putting one school down won't increase your chance of getting a place there, and you risk being offered an unpopular school that's miles away.

2) List your choices in order of preference.

3) Pick at least one school that you have a high chance of getting a place at.

4) Don't leave any blanks on the form.

Stay positive even if you don't get your first choice...

If you're not happy with the school place offered, you should still accept it so you don't run the risk of having no place come September. In the meantime, check your local authority website to find out how to put your child on the waiting lists for your preferred schools. You can also look into whether you have grounds for an appeal.

Preparing your Child for Secondary School

Leaving their cosy primary school to start secondary school is a huge milestone for your child. It's normal to worry about how they'll cope, but there are things you can do to help the transition go smoothly.

Start developing their independence in Year 6

In the <u>final term</u> of <u>primary school</u>, get them to:

- <u>Pack their own bag</u> (ideally the night before). They'll have to remember their PE kit, packed lunch and homework, etc.
- <u>Walk to and from school</u>, or to an agreed place, if the full distance is too far.
- Create a <u>homework schedule</u> so they're prepared to cope with increased homework at secondary school.

Finn's bag felt a little heavier than usual today.

Help your child feel confident with their new routine

Practise their <u>journey</u> to school. Make sure they know what to do if they <u>miss their bus</u>.

Encourage them to display their <u>timetable</u> prominently at home somewhere.

If <u>induction visits</u> to the school are offered, be sure to <u>accept</u>. These days should help them feel <u>excited</u> about starting secondary.

Get them to try their <u>uniform</u> on a couple of times — especially if they're learning to tie a <u>tie</u> for the first time. They'll need to be quick at <u>changing for PE</u> too.

If they're going to be <u>letting themselves in</u> when they get home, get them to <u>practise</u> using their <u>keys</u>.

Remind them of the importance of making <u>sensible food choices</u> at lunch times.

Ensure they have a <u>suitable place</u> at home to do their <u>homework</u> and store their <u>books</u>.

Make sure your child has a suitable <u>school bag</u>. They'll have to carry <u>heavy books</u> and <u>sports kit</u> to school and back — and possibly around with them all day.

Think about how to stop them forgetting or losing their key — attaching it to the inside of their bag with a long string is one method of making sure they always have it.

If they're offered a locker, they'll probably be expected to pay a fee, and maybe even provide their own padlock.

Their primary school will help too

1) Primary school teachers will talk to the children about any <u>worries</u> they might have and give them <u>strategies</u> for coping with <u>problems</u>.
2) Your child's teacher will <u>pass on relevant information</u> to the secondary school about your child before they start there.

A giant leap for your child (and for you)...

Remember, although it can be a worrying time, it's also an exciting time. Secondary schools offer lots more opportunities for children to broaden their horizons, experience new things and widen their circle of friends.

Index

Index

Acknowledgements

Clipart from Corel®

Graphics on pages 5, 32 and 33 © www.edu-clips.com

Photo adapted on page 67 (The River Coquet) © Philip Halling. Licensed for re-use under the Creative Commons Attribution-ShareAlike 2.0 Generic (CC BY-SA 2.0) http://creativecommons.org/licenses/by-sa/2.0/

Images on page 83 iStock.com/TopVectors

Apple is a trademark of Apple Inc., registered in the U.S. and other countries

Google Family Link™ and Google Earth™ are trademarks of Google LLC and this book is not endorsed by or affiliated with Google in any way.

Microsoft® PowerPoint® and Word are trademarks of Microsoft group companies.

Top 10 Tips for Primary School Parents

Here are some mega-important tips for surviving those primary years without becoming a gibbering wreck.

- Keep on top of announcements from school.

- Enjoy the time when your child is little.

- Don't be scared of the teachers.

- Don't compare yourself to other parents.

- 5 minutes a day of reading makes a difference.

- Get involved in school life, e.g. go to the bingo night. But give yourself a break. You can't do everything.

- Encourage your child to try extra-curricular clubs.

- Put name labels on absolutely everything.

- Keep the school informed about things that are happening at home that may affect your child.

- Put spare socks in their bag in case they get wet.

XHHC21